Dreams

Dreams

New and future titles in the series include:

Alien Abductions

Angels

Atlantis

The Bermuda Triangle

The Curse of King Tut

Dragons

ESP

Extinction of the Dinosaurs

Extraterrestrial Life

Fairies

Fortune Telling

Ghosts

Haunted Houses

The Kennedy Assasination

King Arthur

The Loch Ness Monster

Pyramids

Stonehenge

UFOs

Unicorns

Vampires

Witches

The Mystery Library

Dreams

Stuart A. Kallen

**LUCENT
BOOKS** ®

THOMSON

━━━━✦━━━━ ™

GALE

San Diego • Detroit • New York • San Francisco • Cleveland • New Haven, Conn. • Waterville, Maine • London • Munich

On Cover: *The Dream*, by Franz Marc (1880–1916).

LIBRARY OF CONGRESS CATALOGING-IN-PUBLICATION DATA

Kallen, Stuart A., 1955–
    Dreams / by Stuart A. Kallen.
       v. cm.—(The Mystery Library)
Includes bibliographical references and index.
Contents: Dream science—Interpreting dreams—Dreams and cultures—Telepathic
dreaming—Dream power.
    ISBN 1-59018-288-X (alk. paper)
1. Children's dreams—Juvenile literature. 2. Dream interpretation—Juvenile literature.
[1. Dreams. 2. Dream interpretation.] I. Title. II. Mystery library (Lucent Books)
    BF1099.C55K35 2004
    154.6'3 — dc21
                                    2003003542

Contents

Foreword

In Shakespeare's immortal play, *Hamlet*, the young Danish aristocrat Horatio has clearly been astonished and disconcerted by his encounter with a ghost-like apparition on the castle battlements. "There are more things in heaven and earth," his friend Hamlet assures him, "than are dreamt of in your philosophy."

Many people today would readily agree with Hamlet that the world and the vast universe surrounding it are teeming with wonders and oddities that remain largely outside the realm of present human knowledge or understanding. How did the universe begin? What caused the dinosaurs to become extinct? Was the lost continent of Atlantis a real place or merely legendary? Does a monstrous creature lurk beneath the surface of Scotland's Loch Ness? These are only a few of the intriguing questions that remain unanswered, despite the many great strides made by science in recent centuries.

Lucent Books' Mystery Library series is dedicated to exploring these and other perplexing, sometimes bizarre, and often disturbing or frightening wonders. Each volume in the series presents the best-known tales, incidents, and evidence surrounding the topic in question. Also included are the opinions and theories of scientists and other experts who have attempted to unravel and solve the ongoing mystery. And supplementing this information is a fulsome list of sources for further reading, providing the reader with the means to pursue the topic further.

The Mystery Library will satisfy every young reader's fascination for the unexplained. As one of history's greatest scientists, physicist Albert Einstein, put it:

> The most beautiful thing we can experience is the mysterious. It is the source of all true art and science. He to whom this emotion is a stranger, who can no longer wonder and stand rapt in awe, is as good as dead: his eyes are closed.

"What We Do in Our Dreams"

Every night nearly every person undergoes the same physical process—the brain sends chemicals to the body that cause breathing to slow down, limbs to become limp, and eyelids to become heavy. Sleep begins and, eventually, dreams occur. The dreams may be happy, sad, confusing, or peaceful. The dreamer, however, is mostly unaware that he or she is even asleep, let alone traveling through the world of dreams. In the morning, the mind awakes to consciousness, and most people remember almost nothing of what happened during the preceding several hours.

People spend about one—third of their lives asleep and one-fifth of that time dreaming. This means a person who is thirty years old has spent ten years of his or her life asleep—and two complete years in that mysterious space often referred to as "dreamtime." During those two years it is likely that the person has flown through the sky, wandered through empty houses, fallen endlessly into black holes, and confronted all types of people, monsters, and demons. It is also possible that the dreamer conceived of a brilliant idea, wrote a joke, story, or song, or was inspired to create some other work of art. If so, the dreamer has joined the ranks of great artists in history who have found insight in their dreams.

In a sense, the land of dreams is the opposite of the waking world, where logic, science, and reality rule. Dreaming frees people from their earthly bonds and takes them to a place where time and space disappear, the dead come alive, and reality is only restricted by the boundaries of the imagination. This allows the dreamer to imagine the improbable and accomplish the impossible.

But the mind can also unleash its deepest fears, leaving the dreamer naked before a crowd, endlessly pursued by villains, spurned by loved ones, or at the center of ruin and chaos. And such nightmares can take place in a universe populated by an unlimited array of hideous monsters, hellhounds, mutants, ogres, and ghouls. Some people, such as author Edgar Allan Poe, have transferred these hellish visions into immortal stories and poetry.

Most people dream nearly two hours each night. Dreaming frees people from the rules of the waking world and allows them to give free reign to the imagination.

Others have been driven mad by their dreamtime hallucinations.

Dreams are as old as humanity. Throughout history dozens of cultures have based their very existence on dream visions and nightmares. People in ancient societies often believed that dreams came from an outside source, and these visions were frequently looked upon as visitations by gods and goddesses. Dreams were thought to be uncanny predicators of the future, as well as warning signs from the deities.

These beliefs changed over the years. By the early twentieth century, psychiatrists such as Sigmund Freud traced the source of dreams to the subconscious mind. Freud believed that in the deepest recesses of the brain, thoughts that are held back while awake can escape during sleep and express a person's true desires. In more recent times, sleep researchers have discovered many physical effects that take place while a person dreams, such as changes in brain-wave patterns and rapid movement of the eyes.

Although science has shed new light on dreams, many mysteries remain: What are dreams? Where do they come from? What role do dreams play in human survival? What do they mean? Such questions have generated hundreds of books, with answers ranging from the scientific to the supernatural. These visions of the unconscious mind have inspired paintings, symphonies, songs, statues, and skyscrapers. They have guided the actions of kings and commoners alike, while provoking joy, sorrow, and even insanity. With such powers attributed to dreams, it is sometimes said that peoples' lives are shaped by them. As German philosopher Friedrich Nietzsche stated; "What we do in our dreams we also do when we are awake: we invent and make up the person we are."[1]

Chapter 1

Dream Science

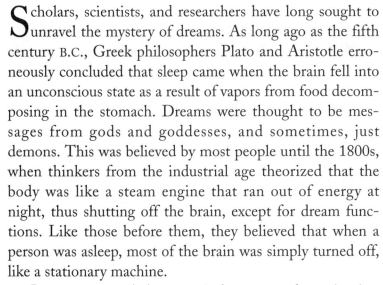

Scholars, scientists, and researchers have long sought to unravel the mystery of dreams. As long ago as the fifth century B.C., Greek philosophers Plato and Aristotle erroneously concluded that sleep came when the brain fell into an unconscious state as a result of vapors from food decomposing in the stomach. Dreams were thought to be messages from gods and goddesses, and sometimes, just demons. This was believed by most people until the 1800s, when thinkers from the industrial age theorized that the body was like a steam engine that ran out of energy at night, thus shutting off the brain, except for dream functions. Like those before them, they believed that when a person was asleep, most of the brain was simply turned off, like a stationary machine.

It was not until the twentieth century that scientists realized that it was the brain that told the body when to sleep. While the body slumbered, the brain was often as active as it was during waking hours, especially when a person was dreaming. This revelation came with the invention of a machine called the electroencephalograph (EEG) in the 1950s. The EEG allowed scientists to measure electrical charges in the brain, called brain waves. When devices that measure electronic activity, called electrodes, are attached to a person's scalp in a lab, the EEG transmits their brain waves to pens that squiggle on sheets of moving paper. Depending on the activity in the brain, the brain waves make the pens move up and down creating common, wavelike patterns. By studying the different kinds of waves, scientists were able to learn that humans undergo five stages of sleep, each marked by a specific brain-wave pattern. With this information, new fields of research began to develop that scientifically explored sleep and dreams.

The Night Journey

During the five stages of sleep, the body undergoes many physical changes. For example, during stage one, sleep, sight,

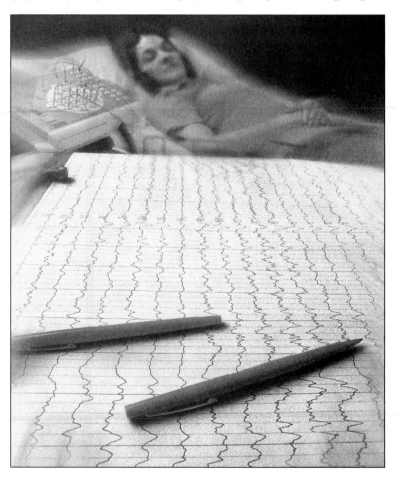

Using an electro-encephalograph, scientists measure a sleeping woman's brain waves. The human brain is as active during sleep as it is during waking hours.

smell, hearing, and other senses shut down. During stage four, muscles are relaxed and the heart and breathing rhythms are slowed. Stage five sleep, when dreams occur, begins a period called rapid eye movement (REM) sleep, when the eyes begin to dart from side to side under closed eyelids. In *The Promise of Sleep*, renowned sleep researcher Dr. William C. Dement writes that during REM, or dream, sleep, a person has "found consciousness once again, but like [a mythical voyager] he is now in a strange land far from the one he inhabits in waking life."[2] At this point, though the body is nearly paralyzed, the brain waves are as active as when a person is fully awake. This mysterious REM stage is so distinctly different from wakefulness and sleep that scientists call it a third state of existence.

This period of dreamtime will last about ten minutes, then the body falls back into deep, stage four sleep. For the rest of the night, the brain will continue to journey between stage four and stage five, with five to ten periods of REM sleep. During these times, a person may experience dozens of dreams. As dawn nears, the REM periods become longer, and the dreams increase. In the hour before wakefulness, the body begins to produce a chemical called cortisol, which releases energy and begins to prepare the person for consciousness.

About eight hours after the brain first fell into unconsciousness, a person opens his eyes and begins the day. The long journey through the night will be completely forgotten, except, possibly, a few dreams, particularly the most recent.

Mysterious Moving Eyeballs

REM sleep was discovered in 1952 by sleep researcher Eugene Aserinsky. By closely observing babies sleeping in their cribs, Aserinsky noticed rapid eye movement under the eyelids. What mystified the researcher was the fact that these REMs took place while the rest of the body was

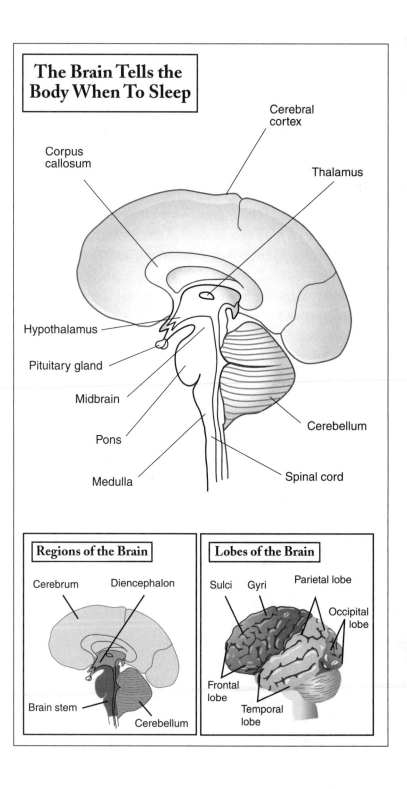

The Brain Tells the Body When To Sleep

Cerebral cortex

Corpus callosum

Thalamus

Hypothalamus

Pituitary gland

Midbrain

Pons

Medulla

Cerebellum

Spinal cord

Regions of the Brain

Cerebrum

Diencephalon

Brain stem

Cerebellum

Lobes of the Brain

Sulci

Gyri

Parietal lobe

Occipital lobe

Frontal lobe

Temporal lobe

completely still. Aserinsky's observation unlocked one of the mysteries about the human body and opened a window on the world of dreams.

Like the brain, eyeball movements emit electrical signals that can be measured with a machine similar to an EEG called an EOG, or electrooculogram. (Ocular means relating to the eye and comes from the Latin *oculus*, or eye.) Aserinsky hooked up an EOG to his eight-year-old son while monitoring his brain waves with an EEG. The researcher observed that during REM sleep, detected with the EOG, his son's brain waves, measured with the EEG, were making wild, jagged paths similar to the waking brain. By observing eyeballs darting rapidly while the dreaming brain was highly active, Aserinsky's discovery contradicted what people commonly believed about the restful nature of sleep.

Over the next few years, Aserinsky, Dement, and Nathaniel Kleitman studied 343 sleeping people in a carefully controlled laboratory setting. By waking their subjects during REM sleep, they discovered that nearly 95 percent of the sleepers were experiencing vivid dreams. Those awakened from non-REM sleep, however, could not remember their dreams.

The sleep researchers also discovered during these tests that physical eye movement can be directly tied to the content of dreams, as Stuart Holroyd writes in *Dream Worlds:*

> In one series of experiments Dr. Dement discovered a direct correspondence between sleepers' eye movements and the images that occurred in their dreams. The tracings from the EEG machine record both vertical [up-and-down] and horizontal [side-to-side] eye movement. A sleeper who was awakened from a dream in which his eyes had been making very rapid horizontal movements said that he had been watching two people throwing tomatoes at each other. Vertical movements occurred when the

dream content involved climbing ladders or stairs. On being awakened from a REM period, one young woman reported dreaming that she walked up some stairs, glancing down at each one in turn, and on reaching the top had walked over a group of people. The experimenter hadn't seen the EEG tracings at the time, but he predicted on the basis of the dream report that they would show a series of vertical upward movements followed by horizontal movements [after she reached the top of the ladder]. The tracings proved him right.[3]

These experiments also showed that although a person may toss and turn in stage four sleep, muscles totally relax and remain still during REM sleep at the same time the brain becomes very active. In fact, a person awakened during REM slumber may experience "sleep paralysis" and be unable to move for a few seconds. In *Nightmares*, Sandra Shulman says that this inability to move "may well account for those horrendous [dreams] of being rooted to the spot while being pursued by some dreadful creatures, or that suffocating sensation of [a wild beast] crouching on the sleeper's chest."[4] Heartbeats and respiratory rates, however, speed up and become slightly irregular even as the body lays nearly immobilized.

Deprived of Dreams

Once sleep researchers had connected dreaming to REM patterns, Dement began to wonder what would happen to a person who was deprived of dreaming. In January 1959, the doctor was able to answer this question by studying a New York disc jockey named Peter Tripp who volunteered to stay awake for two hundred hours—eight days and eight hours—in a stunt to raise money for the March of Dimes charity.

While Tripp broadcast his "Wakeathon" from a glass-enclosed booth in Times Square in New York City, Dement and others observed and recorded his actions. Whenever Tripp began to fall asleep, doctors shook him awake, joked with him, played games with him, and gave him tests to take. After about three days, Tripp began to act as if he were drunk, laughing hysterically at things that were not funny and reacting belligerently to imaginary insults. The DJ also began experiencing paranoid delusions and hallucinations, seeing cobwebs, mice, and kittens, and thinking that the doctor's suit was made of slithering worms. He ransacked drawers for money that was not there and believed that a technician had dropped a hot electrode into his shoe. These hallucinations intensified between midnight and 8 A.M.—the time when Tripp was normally asleep and dreaming.

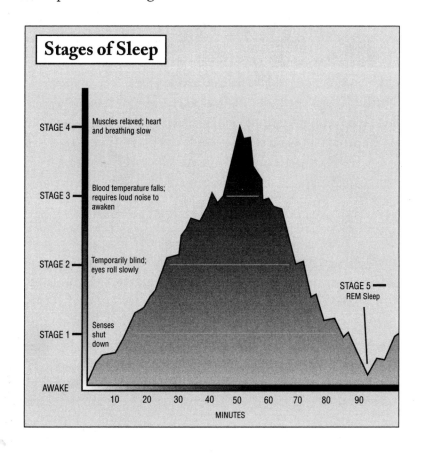

Stages of Sleep

STAGE 4 — Muscles relaxed; heart and breathing slow

STAGE 3 — Blood temperature falls; requires loud noise to awaken

STAGE 2 — Temporarily blind; eyes roll slowly

STAGE 5 — REM Sleep

STAGE 1 — Senses shut down

AWAKE

10   20   30   40   50   60   70   80   90

MINUTES

After 201 hours, Tripp finally went to sleep. During this time he experienced REM sleep about 28 percent of the time, nearly 50 percent more than the average time spent dreaming. Interestingly, Tripp's body needed only thirteen hours of sleep after being awake for days, but the brain needed to make up for the dreamtime missed. Doctors concluded from this experiment that for some mysterious reason, dreams, even more than sleep, are essential for mental health.

In order to confirm his belief that people needed to dream more than they needed to sleep, Dement experimented with volunteers. For five consecutive nights, subjects were awakened every time they entered REM sleep. On each following night, the volunteers entered REM periods more often, until the fifth night, when they experienced REM sleep an average of twenty times, or about four times more than normal.

By contrast, a group of volunteers were awakened as often, but during non-REM periods. These test subjects experienced no increase in REM episodes. This led researchers to the conclusion that for some unexplainable reason, the brain needs to dream. As Holroyd writes:

> Perhaps the most overwhelming fact . . . is that we must dream. Our bodies apparently require dreaming with the same urgency that they demand food and drink, and any person who is deprived of dreams suffers as severely as a person who has been starved.[5]

Dement's research exposed other mysterious facts about dreams. Although it was previously believed that dreams lasted only a few seconds and were, in a sense, sensational dramas played out in rapid-fire succession, researchers discovered that dreams may take place in real time. In fact, some subjects reenacted stories that lasted up to twenty minutes.

Research also showed that, in all probability, all people dream every night, and this most often takes place during periods of REM sleep. Those who say they never remember their dreams are also dreaming nightly, but for unknown reasons have extreme difficulty remembering them when they wake up.

Lucid Dreaming

In the late 1970s, Dement and his colleague Stephen LaBerge began to research lucid dreaming, a peculiar phenomenon in which people become aware that they are having a dream, and can consciously alter the content of that dream while they are asleep. In this way, according to Dement, lucid dreamers "report that they can make themselves fly through walls and over houses, that they are able to practice the piano, take vacations to specific locales, and arrange sexual encounters, all while deep in REM sleep."[6]

LaBerge had experienced lucid dreams since childhood and wanted to find the specific scientific reasons for such dreams. In experiments, LaBerge slept hooked up to an

EEG in a lab. Remarkably, LaBerge was able to consciously move his eyeballs in a specific prearranged pattern—left-right, left-right, right-left—different from the usual REMs, which he could use as a signal to tell researchers when he was having a lucid dream. When this happened, Dement woke LaBerge and took reports about the dreams.

Over the course of these experiments, the researchers discovered that only one in five people experience lucid dreams naturally, though some have short moments of lucidity right before awakening. But LaBerge also concluded that up to 60 percent of test subjects were able to experience lucid dreaming with practice and training—by simply saying repeatedly at bedtime, "I *will* have a lucid dream."[7]

To teach others to dream lucidly, LaBerge developed a special visor that projected a blinking red light onto a subject's eyelids at the time REM sleep was occurring. This signal, bright enough to pass through the eyelids, cues the dreamers to make conscious attempts to manipulate their dreams. LaBerge also developed a specific mind training technique, known as the Mnemonic Induction of Lucid Dreams (MILD), that allows subjects, with practice, to have up to twenty lucid dreams a month.

As his work continued, LaBerge gained an amazing control over his body as he dreamed. In addition to signaling to researchers with specific eye movements, he learned a method of clenching his hands to deliver messages about his dreams in Morse code, in which letters of the alphabet are represented by various sequences of dots and dashes or short and long signals. With this ability, LaBerge was able, possibly for the first time in history, to communicate his dreams to researchers as they unfolded.

By breaking down the wall between the unconscious dream state and the waking mind, LaBerge and others who learned his methods could accurately relate what was happening in their dreams while it was happening. LaBerge recorded his experiences and methods in the 1985 book

Animal Dreams

Animals have a wide variety of sleep patterns. Lions may slumber for two to three days at a time, while some antelope sleep only one hour a day. Dolphins sleep while they swim by resting one half of their brain for about two hours while the other half remains alert to danger. But all mammals, whether they live on land or in the sea, experience REM sleep. Researchers have long wondered if animals have dreams that are similar to those experienced by humans.

In 2001, researchers at the Massachusetts Institute of Technology (MIT) believed they found an answer to that question. By monitoring the brain waves of rats while they were learning tasks, researchers used EEGs to isolate the parts of the brain used for memory. During REM sleep, the rats showed brain waves similar to those recorded during training. This led researchers to the conclusion that animals may have complex dreams that recall sequences of events that happened when they were awake. And, like humans, animals—from rats to lions—may be able to use dreams to recall and evaluate their life experiences in order to help them get through their days.

All animals experience REM sleep. Scientists believe that animals may have dreams as complex as human dreams.

Lucid Dreaming. The success of this book generated great media interest in lucid dreaming and inspired people to learn the techniques for such dreams themselves.

While many simply want to have unrestricted fun in their dreams, LaBerge's techniques have also been used to cure those who have reoccurring nightmares. Researchers suggest that by taking control of their dreams, those who suffer nightmares can learn to banish them. As LaBerge writes, lucid dreams are "a priceless treasure that belongs to each of us. This treasure, the ability to dream lucidly, gives us the opportunity . . . to overcome limitations, fears, and nightmares, to explore our minds, to enjoy incredible adventure, and to discover transcendent consciousness."[8]

Dream Theories

While LaBerge studied lucid dreams as a way to change lives, other researchers have been trying to discover why people dream at all. Some doctors believe that dreaming is a psychological necessity. It acts as a "safety valve" used to prevent the brain from experiencing insanity. Others believe that dreaming is merely a physical need based on repairing the wear and tear a body goes through every day.

Dr. Ian Oswald of Edinburgh University in Scotland, for example, theorizes that dreams might be a result of chemicals the body uses to repair itself during the night. Oswald noticed that during non-REM sleep, the human body releases a chemical called human growth hormone (HGH) into the blood that repairs bones and muscles, weary from a day's activities. But during REM sleep, the body temporarily stops producing these hormones. Oswald believes that for some inexplicable reason, dreaming draws these important hormones into the brain where they repair the neurons and synapses that make the organ function.

Scientists Francis Crick and Graeme Mitchison, on the other hand, think dreaming is the brain's way of preventing insanity. These men believe that the brain experiences so much stimulus during waking hours that it must find a way to process this information without becoming overloaded. Instead of "crashing" like a computer, the dreaming brain processes strange and unnecessary thoughts into harmless images, most of which are forgotten in the morning. In *Our Dreaming Mind*, dream researcher Robert Van de Castle describes the theory put forth by Crick and Mitchison:

> During REM sleep . . . the brain attempts to rid itself of excessive memory . . . [which is] the reverse of . . . learning. This insures that the brain will not accumu-

late too much useless clutter. These researchers state that memory is stored in neural [nerve] nets and that there is a limit to what these nets can store before the system begins to "misbehave." If we remember our dreams too frequently, they will interfere with this process of unclogging the [nerve nets], and presumably could have negative consequences for our well-being. . . . Thus, Crick and Mitchison argue, "We dream in order to forget" . . . "we dream to reduce fantasy," or "we dream to reduce obsession."[9]

Other researchers contradict this theory, saying that the brain uses dreaming for functions more creative than simply erasing harmful thoughts. They point out that dreaming has inspired poets, painters, and others to imagine great works of art. As dream researcher J. Allan Hobson writes: "During REM sleep, the brain and mind seem to be engaging in a process of fantastic creation. Thus new ideas and new feelings, and new views of old problems, can be expected to arise within dreams. These may be carried forward into the conscious mind or remain unconscious as part of our deeper creative [process]."[10]

Some researchers doubt that dreams either clear or clutter the mind. Instead they theorize that the stage-five REM sleep experienced during dreams is based on the ancient need for survival; this period of light sleep originally allowed people to awaken quickly if threatened by wild animals or aggressive enemies.

Nightmare Research

Fear and dread can often haunt a person's dreamworld. Such frightening dreams are called nightmares after the Old English word *mares*, which means goblins. A nightmare can be so dramatic that a person can sweat profusely and experience a pounding heart and labored breathing.

Five Aspects of Dreaming

J. Allan Hobson is a neuroscientist who has studied brain structure and dreams. In *The Dreaming Universe* by Fred Alan Wolf, Hobson lists five characteristics common to dreaming:

1. Strong emotions—so strong that they even tend to [end] or interrupt the dream.

2. Illogical content and organization wherein the usual aspects of time and space and even identification of persons, as well as the natural laws of physics, are suspended.

3. The experience of . . . sensory impressions regardless of how bizarre those experiences are.

4. The uncritical acceptance of those . . . sensory experiences as if those experiences were perfectly normal everyday occurrences even though they are bizarre and strange.

5. The difficulty of remembering any dream unless the dreamer attempts to record the dream immediately upon awakening.

Dreams often involve illogical scenarios that the dreamer accepts as normal.

Some dreamers awaken with a scream and find it difficult to get back to sleep.

Researchers have determined that nightmares most often take place during the later parts of the night, when REM sleep is longest, but why people have them remains a mystery. Some psychiatrists believe that they act as a way for people to visualize the subconscious fears and problems they experience—but refuse to think about—during the day.

This might be why people often dream that they are falling or being chased or shot at. Such fears spill out in dreams, possibly so that a person can confront or deal with them.

While almost everyone has an occasional nightmare, a study by psychiatrist Ernest Hartmann showed that people who are more emotionally sensitive, and who work in artistic occupations, tend to experience bad dreams more often. In one of the most comprehensive studies of nightmares ever conducted, Hartmann gathered a group of fifty adult volunteers who had been troubled by frequent nightmares since childhood. While the nightmares had common themes, such as being chased by monsters or large groups of soldiers such as Nazis, Hartmann also discovered similarities among the dreamers. According to dream researcher Robert Van de Castle:

> None of the nightmare sufferers held ordinary blue- or white-collar jobs. They frequently had musical or artistic careers or were teachers. They also did not fit society's sex-role stereotypes: there was not a single tough, macho man or a woman who saw her role as marrying and having children. Their personal relationships were often stormy, and they tended to become overinvolved in relationships quickly, which then led to difficult, painful separations. Adolescent years had been particularly difficult for them and one third of them had attempted suicide or had thought very seriously about it. Two thirds of them had sought psychotherapy some time in their lives.[11]

Hartmann did not answer the question as to whether nightmares caused the personality problems or psychological difficulties caused frequent nightmares. Research has shown, however, that depressed people experience longer periods of REM sleep, so it may be possible that, for reasons unknown, excessively long dreams and frequent nightmares may be harmful to mental health.

Whether dreams affect life or life affects dreams, about 11 percent of the population suffers from reoccurring nightmares. These episodes often leave the dreamer feeling weak and powerless. As John E. Mack writes in *Nightmares and Human Conflict*:

> Whether the dreamer is threatened by an ancient demon, a vampire, a lobster, a fairy story monster, a robot, or an atomic ray, his experience is in each instance like that of a helpless child confronted by powerful forces with which he is unable to deal effectively.[12]

Night Terrors

Dreamers having nightmares may shake off the usual paralysis of REM sleep and attempt to run, jerking their limbs as they slumber. However, extreme physical reactions may be experienced if a dreamer is having what is known as a night terror.

Night terrors occur during the deep, stage four, non-REM sleep and often cause sleepers to bolt upright in panic and let out terrified shrieks. Unlike those waking up from night-

Artists and emotionally sensitive people tend to experience nightmares more often than other people. Scientists are still uncertain why people have nightmares.

mares, who often remember what they were dreaming, people with night terrors wake up confused, disoriented, and drowsy, rarely remembering the dream. And unlike nightmares, which are based on psychological fears, night terrors may be related to physical problems that occur during sleep, such as breathing difficulties, accidentally choking on saliva, or even an arm or leg that has become inadvertently twisted. This explains why people commonly feel that they are gasping, being crushed, or choking during night terrors.

While nightmares can last up to ten minutes, night terrors are over in a matter of one or two minutes. During that short period of time, the pulse and respiratory rates can double in seconds. If the terror does not wake a person, he or she might begin sleepwalking. Night terrors are most common in children and tend to disappear as a person grows older.

"Simply Enjoy Them"

While night terrors and nightmares are the most upsetting sleep events, many dreams are emotionally neutral or even joyous. While researchers continue to form complicated scientific hypotheses about the basis of dreams, others suggest that they may be reading too much into them. As Hobson writes:

> Why can't dreams include the function of being entertaining? Why should we always be looking below decks, fore and aft, to understand . . . the purpose of these delightful home movies? Why can't we accept the [creative] function of dreams as something given to us . . . for our own pleasure? And might not such enhancement of our pleasure—and our self-esteem—even contribute to more successful functioning as human beings? . . . Dreams are truly marvelous. Why not simply enjoy them?[13]

Chapter 2

Interpreting Dreams

Dreams can be baffling, bizarre, frightening, funny, or silly—sometimes all at once. Often these nighttime dramas seem to contain messages, warnings, or symbolic tales. This has prompted philosophers, scientists, doctors, and religious leaders throughout history to give great significance to the imagery that appears in dreams.

Dream images are believed to have played an important role in spirituality and mythology since the dawn of humanity. Researchers speculate that prehistoric drawings of animal-human creatures painted on the walls of French caves twenty thousand years ago were inspired by dreams and created for religious reasons. These dream-images, etched into stone by some ancient artist, might have been interpreted to mean good luck in hunting or war. From the days of the cave dwellers until the nineteenth century A.D., many people believed that dreams were baffling supernatural messages from gods and demons and that only shamans, oracles, and other religious soothsayers were skilled enough to interpret their meaning. While most skeptics do not believe that dreams contain any hidden meaning, today dream interpretation remains a popular topic of books, movies, and even TV shows.

Ancient Dream Diviners

The first evidence of dream analysis appeared around seven thousand years ago in Mesopotamia, located in present-day

Iraq. The ancient Mesopotamian culture of Sumerians, Babylonians, and Assyrians developed the first formalized system of writing called cuneiform, utilizing more then seven hundred symbols that were carved into clay tablets. Some of these tablets contain dream imagery as deciphered by ancient shamans. These interpretations provide insight into the types of dreams experienced in the ancient world. For example, people often dreamed of such basics as eating. In the second millennia B.C. the clay tablet now known as *The Babylonian-Assyrian Dream Book* advised: "If [a man dreams that he] eats the meat of some wild animal [he will experience] evil seizure, there will be cases of death in his family." However, dreams of cannibalism seem to bring good luck: "If he eats human meat, he will know great riches." Mysteriously, "If he eats the flesh of his [own] foot his eldest son will die."[14]

Dreams of flying seem to have been nearly as common as dreams of eating. *The Babylonian-Assyrian Dream Book* assigns different meanings to such dreams, depending on

Ancient Mesopotamians recorded dream imagery on clay tablets like this one. People have analyzed dreams throughout history.

the situation and the status of the person who has the dream:

> If [a man has wings and] takes off and flies once, [if he is an] important person his good luck [will vanish: if he is] a commoner his bad luck will leave him: if he is thrown into jail he will leave the jail . . . if he is sick he will become well again. . . .
>
> If [a man who is flying] sinks into a river and emerges again, this man will have riches. If he [flies] into a river in his clothes, the foundation of this man is solid. If he falls into a river and moves upstream, he will ask something from a person who is not friendly to him and he will give it to him. . . . If he [flies] into a river and comes up again, he will have worries. If he crosses a river, he will experience confusion.[15]

Egyptian Men of the Magic Library

The ancient Egyptians shared a similar interest in deciphering dream imagery. In fact, the Egyptians elevated this practice to a science called oneiromancy, or dream interpretation. Since they believed that dreams were supernatural messages from the deities, they constructed dozens of temples where people from all levels of society could go to have their dreams interpreted.

Each temple contained libraries with papyrus scrolls, called *omina*, that contained precise meanings for specific dream imagery. The Egyptians believed that these scrolls had been dictated by the gods and were therefore sacred. One of the oldest such *omina*, called *Dream Book*, was written around 2000 B.C. This papyrus lists more than one hundred dreams; "good" or lucky dreams were written in black, while "bad" or ill-fated dreams were in red. An excerpt from the *Dream Book* states:

If a man sees himself in a dream—

.....dead—good omen, meaning long life

.....eating crocodile flesh—good omen, meaning he will become a village official

.....bringing in cattle—good omen, dreamer will evangelize the spirit of the community

.....plunging into cold waters—good omen, indicating absolution of all ills

.....with his face in a mirror—bad omen, meaning a new [way of life must be undertaken]

.....uncovering his own backside—bad omen, he will become an orphan

.....putting one's face to the ground—bad omen, meaning the dead want something[16]

The ancient Egyptians recorded the meanings of their dreams on papyrus scrolls. They believed that dreams came from the gods and were therefore sacred.

Such omens were studied by professional dream interpreters, called Learned Men of the Magic Library. These oracles made their services open to the general public, who would pay them to explain their dreams. The Learned Men advertised their business on signs outside the temples with slogans such as: "I interpret dreams, having the gods' mandate to do so; good luck."[17]

People who wanted to gain the most knowledge from their dreams would sleep at the temple after practicing various religious tasks, such as fasting, praying, and performing magical rites. Upon awakening, Learned Men of the Magic Library would interpret the client's dreams. If someone could not personally attend, he could send a surrogate, usually a servant, to perform the dream work instead.

The Interpretation of Dreams

In later years, around the fourth century B.C., the classical Greeks utilized techniques similar to Egyptian dream interpretation, but changed the messages to fit with their own culture. The Greeks, for example, believed that dreams were messages from the father of the gods, Zeus. The winged messenger Hermes was said to deliver these messages to people who sometimes consulted soothsayers to interpret them as sources of inspiration, advice, prophecies, and warnings. These were often written down, and by the second century B.C., the Greeks had logged the meaning of countless dreams. Around that time, an author and professional dream diviner named Artemidorus compiled these night visions, along with his own analysis and interpretations, into a dream dictionary called *Oneirocritica (The Interpretation of Dreams)*, which became one of the most famous books of ancient times.

The *Oneirocritica*, still published today, contains three thousand dreams in five volumes. Each volume is extremely exhaustive. For example, Volume One lists eighty-two dreams about the human body, covering topics from the head to the toe, including hair, eyes, forehead, tongue, neck, chest, genitals, knees, ankles, and so on. Concerning dreams about the nose—or two noses—Artemidorus writes:

> Dreaming that one has a handsome and well-shaped nose is auspicious [favorable] for all men. For it is a sign of great sensitivity, foresight in one's affairs, and the acquaintance of good men. For men inhale better air through the nose and derive profit from it. But to [dream of having] no nose signifies [stupidity] and the hatred of prominent people as well as death to the sick. For the skulls of the dead are found without noses. To have two noses signifies discord with one's family and relations.[18]

Artemidorus also deciphers the meaning behind dreams that feature natural phenomenon, such as fire, water, weather, animals, and dozens of Greek gods. Dreams about physical activities, such as tanning leather, boxing, and blowing a trumpet, are covered, while an entire section exists for dreaming about food. In this section, Artemidorus writes that dreaming about radishes can "indicate that secrets will be revealed," while pumpkin dreams expose "vain hopes."[19]

Some of the dreams Artemidorus discusses are quite bizarre, such as visions of flying ants or dreaming about eating one's own flesh (for a poor man, this indicates good luck because the flesh represents profits in business).

The classical Greeks believed that dreams were messages sent by Zeus.

Dreams about death fill many pages of *The Interpretation of Dreams*. Artemidorus notes that, often, such dreams mean the opposite of what they seem to. For example, dreaming of being hit by lightning is good because "no one who has been struck by a thunderbolt is without fame [and he may be] revered even as a god."[20] For a slave to dream of death means he may gain his freedom because "a dead man has no master and is free from toil and service."[21]

Artemidorus claims that there are two types of dreams; those that will come true as seen and those that disclose their meaning through riddles. The author advises that to properly decipher dreams, one needs to know the dreamer's occupation, birth, financial status, state of health, and age. The dream interpreter should also travel widely and learn as much about the world as possible so that he will have the perspective necessary to interpret the dreams of slaves, farmers, wealthy merchants, and others.

Finally, the author analyzes ninety-five actual dreams that he had heard over the year. These examples are used by the author as a way of proving cause and effect, that is, showing that a dream really did predict the future. When a man went blind, for example, Artemidorus traced the problem to a dream the man had before he was afflicted:

> Someone dreamt that he kindled a lamp from the moon. He [soon] went blind, because he took his light from a source from which it is impossible to kindle a fire and especially because the moon is said to have no light of its own.[22]

"Endless Imbecilities"?

The interpretations made by Artemidorus were used as a basis for dream analysis for centuries. Despite this general acceptance, some people have been extremely skeptical about dream interpretation. The Roman philosopher Cicero, who lived in the first century B.C., was one such

Carl Jung's Dream Theories

Swiss psychotherapist Carl Jung was a prominent dream researcher, a colleague of Freud's. Jung, born in 1875, studied under Freud for five years, beginning in 1907, but the two doctors had strong disagreements that led to a bitter rivalry.

Jung believed that dreams could not only help a patient understand his or her troubles, but could also reveal a creative answer to fix the problem. The doctor developed this theory when he realized that there were common dream symbols that ran across different cultures throughout the centuries. These symbols fell into categories Jung labeled the hero, monster, mother, father, sacrifice, and mask, and which appeared in the dreams of everyone regardless of their background. This led Jung to develop the theory known as the "collective unconscious," that identifies a part of the mind not dependent upon personal experiences, but rather on symbols and images from ancient times woven into the brains of all people.

Jung believed that some dream images came from the collective unconscious and could be analyzed as paths to self-awareness and self-fulfillment. For Jung, the unconscious did not merely focus on crude instincts such as hunger, sex, and survival but also contained the secret of life's meaning, which was hidden from the conscious mind. Jung believed that dreams would reveal that secret during slumber.

disbeliever who dismissed dream interpreters as frauds who took advantage of peoples' insecurities. Cicero wrote:

> Let us reject . . . this divination of dreams . . . For, to speak truly, that superstition has extended itself through all nations, and has oppressed the intellectual energies of all men, and has betrayed them into endless imbecilities.[23]

Cicero, apparently, held a minority opinion because the writings of Artemidorus remained popular hundreds of years after his death. In fact, in the 1400s, after Johannes Gutenberg invented the first printing press, the second book he printed, after the Bible, was Artemidorus's *The Interpretation of Dreams.*

In the following years, printers sold tens of thousands of dream dictionaries based on the words of Artemidorus. These simple books allowed the general public, for the first time, to

Dreams of the Ancients

In ancient times, the pronouncements of dream interpreters were considered messages handed down from the gods. Therefore they were accurate and correct, beyond doubt. However, analysis of those interpretations shows that similar dreams meant different things in different cultures. In *Dream Worlds*, Stuart Holroyd provides some examples:

Birds

Greek: Birds symbolize types of people—for example, eagles stand for men and women in power, pigeons for wicked women.

Assyrian: To meet up with a bird in a dream is a sign that the dreamer will recover some belonging that had been lost.

Hebrew: To have a dream with an owl in it symbolizes bad luck. However, to dream of any other kind of bird means good luck.

Egyptian: When a dreamer catches a bird of any kind in a dream, it means that he or she will lose some possessions.

Snakes

Greek: A dream of a snake forebodes sickness or presence of enemies. If it is a powerful snake, it means severe illness.

Assyrian: If the dreamer seizes a snake in a dream, it foretells that an angel will give protection to the dreamer.

Hebrew: A snake means an assured livelihood. A snake bite puts security in doubt. To kill a snake means a lost livelihood.

Egyptian: To have a dream in which a snake appears is considered lucky because it means that a dispute will be settled.

Trees

Greek: It is good luck for carpenters and mariners to dream of trees whose wood is used for shipmaking, but bad luck for others.

Assyrian: If the dreamer cuts down a date palm in a dream, it is a good omen that his or her problems will be well solved.

Hebrew: A dream in which there is a palm tree is a warning to the one who dreams it that punishment for sins will come.

Egyptian: To sit on the limb of a tree in a dream has the happy meaning that the dreamer's troubles will soon be overcome.

give meaning to their own dreams without consulting diviners, seers, priests, and Learned Men of the Magic Library. Today, such books remain popular. As Sandra Shulman writes, "The paperback dream manuals, available at any bookstand, are the mass-produced descendants of Babylonian and Assyrian clay tables, describing dreams and nightmares and giving interpretations, that date back to 5000 B.C."[24]

Dr. Freud's Royal Road

By the late eighteenth century, people began rejecting the notion that dreams were mysterious messages handed down from the gods. This was during a period known as the Age of Enlightenment, when belief in science and rational thought began to replace ancient superstitions. Philosophers and scholars, when writing about dreams, began to connect them to the individual's unconscious thoughts and desires. As British essayist William Hazlitt wrote in the early 1800s, in dreams "things come upon us in unexpected revelation, which we keep out of our thoughts at other times. . . . [We] may discover our . . . unconscious sentiments, with respect to persons and things. . . . We are not hypocrites in our sleep. The curb is taken off from our passions and imagination wanders at will."[25]

Taking a cue from Hazlitt, scholars began to attribute dreams to thoughts that are repressed, that is, images of a sexual, violent, or unpleasant nature that are blocked from the conscious mind and relegated to the subconscious. For example, if someone sees a horrible accident, she may refuse to think about it while awake, but have nightmares about it when sleeping.

By the late nineteenth century, an Austrian-born doctor named Sigmund Freud began working with such theories and founded psychoanalysis, a method of treating mental illness. Freud believed that mental problems could be traced to repressed childhood experiences, particularly to suppressed sexual desires.

Many of Freud's first patients were young women who suffered from hysteria, a mysterious illness that can cause amnesia, vomiting, blindness, and paralysis for no apparent reason. Freud believed that he could help these women, and find the root causes of their hysteria, by getting them to talk freely about their past experiences and childhood memories. But the psychologist quickly discovered that the fastest way to reveal repressed trauma was to have his patients tell him about their dreams. By analyzing the dream imagery, Freud believed he could bring to light buried memories, fears, and desires.

In 1900, Freud published his theories concerning dream research in the groundbreaking book also titled *The Interpretation of Dreams*. With little modesty, Freud called his dream book the "royal road to . . . unconscious activities of the mind."[26] While writing about many of his patient's dreams in detail, Freud puts forth the theory that dream imagery is often based on wish fulfillment, that is, realizing subconscious wishes and desires that even the conscious mind did not know existed.

Analyze This

According to Freud there are four types of wish-fulfillment dreams. The simplest dreams are based on waking wishes that are left unfulfilled. For example, Freud writes of his eight-year-old son who wished that he could ride in a horse-drawn chariot after reading an exciting book about Greek mythology. That night the little boy dreamed that he was flying through the sky in such a chariot accompanied by a Greek god. A second type of wish-fulfillment dream comes from the desire of the sleeping body to relieve physical stresses, such as thirst. In *The Interpretation of Dreams*, Freud provides his own dream as an example:

> If, in the evening, I eat anchovies, olives, or other strongly salted foods, I am thirsty at night, and

therefore I wake. The waking, however, is preceded by a dream, which has always the same content, namely, that I am drinking. I am drinking long draughts of water, it tastes as delicious as only a cool drink can taste when one's throat is parched; and then I wake, and find that I have an actual desire to drink. The cause of this dream is thirst, which I perceive when I wake. From this sensation arises the wish to drink, and the dream shows me this wish as fulfilled.[27]

Freud also considers other dreams to represent more sinister wish-fulfillment. These would include dreams in which people murder their spouses or bosses. Such dreams indicate that the dreamer harbors deep resentment toward the person he murders in dreams.

The fourth type of wish-fulfillment dreams is based on subconscious desires so vile that the dreamer normally does not allow them to break into conscious thought. Such dreams often contain bizarre and perverted images and situations usually of the sexual nature.

Analyzing such dreams led Freud to deduce that nearly every dream image revolved around a combination of three basic concepts: bodily functions, suppressed childhood anger toward parents, and sexual repression. Even seemingly straightforward dreams fell into this category. For example, people commonly have dreams about ghosts or burglars. The average person might surmise that, because these images are frightening, they might readily appear as

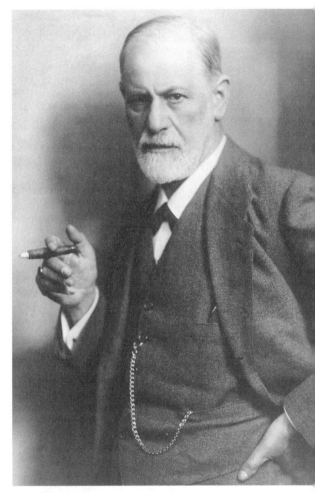

Dr. Sigmund Freud treated his patients by analyzing their dreams. His method is known as psychoanalysis.

nightmares. Freud, however, attributes these images to childhood, negative feelings toward parents, and even wetting the bed:

> Robbers, burglars and ghosts . . . who sometimes pursue their victims after they are asleep, all originate from . . . [early childhood] reminiscence. [Ghosts and robbers represent parents] who rouse children and [wake] them up to prevent their wetting their bed. . . . The robbers [stand] for the sleeper's father, whereas the ghosts corresponded to [mothers] in white night-gowns.[28]

Freud theorized that ghosts or burglars in dreams represent parents who wake sleeping children. Freud believed that many dreams stem from childhood trauma.

Over the years, intense debate has raged around such analysis. Some have claimed that Freud was a genius who changed the way people decipher the meaning of dreams. Others condemn Freud for equating nearly every dream

with sexual repression and childhood trauma. They also criticize psychoanalysis by pointing out that some mental illnesses result from chemical imbalances in the brain, and could never be cured simply by analyzing bad dreams. As Robert Todd Carroll writes on The Skeptic's Dictionary website:

> Would you treat a broken leg or diabetes . . . by interpreting the patient's dreams? Of course not. . . . [The] interpretation of dreams . . . [is not open to] scientific formulation or empirical testing . . . [but a] blank check to speculate at will without any check in reality.[29]

Despite such criticism, psychoanalysis through dream interpretation has evolved since the publication of Freud's innovative and influential book. Today, it is a widespread and respected part of many programs used to treat mental illnesses.

Common Dream Scenes

While some use psychologists and psychiatrists to help them analyze their dreams, millions of people interpret their own dreams every day using some of the hundreds of dream dictionaries found in bookstores and libraries. These books may contain information gleaned from ancient Egyptian superstition, the writings of Artemidorus, Freudian dream analysis, or simply the personal opinions of the authors. Whatever the source, many of the dreams analyzed in these books are so common, since they are based on universal experiences and fears, that almost every book has them. Such dreams include falling, flying, appearing naked in public, and being unprepared for some important task.

Psychologists believe that falling dreams can be traced back to early childhood, when the first uncertain efforts to walk are undertaken. Although most people cannot remember that period in their lives, such theories state that deeply held fears from that time remain forever alive in the unconscious mind. Others theorize that falling represents a feeling of failure, that the dreamer has "fallen down" on the job or at school.

The meaning of flying dreams seems to be more elusive. Those who believe in supernatural forces beyond human understanding think that flying dreams are a sort of out-of-body experience called astral projection in which the soul leaves the body and travels through space. Psychologists believe that flying represents a person who is happy, that is "flying high," and who is achieving her dreams. Freud, unsurprisingly, associated flying dreams with sexual desire.

Dreams of nakedness, on the other hand, are not often associated with sex. Instead, people who dream that they are naked in public are said to be expressing subconscious feelings of shame, fear, vulnerability, and anxiety. Seen in a more positive light, nudity could symbolize feelings of freedom, honesty, and openness. Freud believed such dreams expressed a longing for the innocence of childhood, before feelings such as modesty and shame were learned.

Being unprepared for a task is common among students, who often dream that they are taking a test for which they have not studied. In such dreams, pencils may break repeatedly, words may appear in strange, unreadable text, and the student may even be naked. Another form of this dream is when a person appears at a podium or on a stage unable to speak or perform. Such dreams are often traceable to real events in the life of the dreamer. Taken the right way, they may prod the student to study or the speaker to learn his lines.

"Painful Torture"

People continue to analyze their dreams because many people regularly experience unpleasant or bizarre dreams. One study cataloged more than ten thousand dreams and found out that 58 percent were associated with sadness, anxiety, or anger, while only 26 percent were described as positively happy. With such findings, it is little wonder that people continue to look for answers to their dreams. However, it remains a matter of debate as to whether modern dream interpretation is any more accurate than that of the Egyptians, Artemidorus, or Freud.

Even in the time of the ancient Greeks, scholars such as Plutarch considered dream analysis an unnecessary—and sometimes dangerous—superstition. Around the first century B.C., Plutarch addressed individuals who were troubled by dream imagery: "The gods have given us sleep for oblivion and respite from troubles, why do you make it a lasting and painful torture for yourself?"[30] Despite such advice, people continue to search for meaning in dreams, even though their meanings can be elusive and mysterious.

Chapter 3

Dreams That Inspire

Throughout history dreams have inspired people and molded cultures in some of the most powerful societies the world has ever known. Dreams have shaped decisions about war, peace, and religion—decisions that have affected the daily lives of billions of people. Dream imagery has also inspired poets, artists, musicians, and others to create works that continue to impact culture today. Some of these dreams, published in the Bible, Koran, and other sacred books, exert a strong influence over the modern world.

Although dreams have played an important role in art, culture, and society throughout time, people in modern Western society generally separate the reality of day-to-day life from the unexplained illusions and images of the dream world. The distinction between reality and dreams, however, has not always been so rigid or well defined. In ancient times, for example, people believed that the world was filled with spirits and demons, gods and goddesses, and forces of good and evil. In such an uncertain world where people lacked the scientific knowledge to explain natural disasters, sickness, death, and other unpredictable events, dreams might reveal potent and mysterious deities who came to grant gifts, reveal messages, and provide warnings. In return, ancient people practiced magic and rituals they had seen in their dreams in order to appease nature, appeal to the gods, and bring good luck.

Decisions Based on Dreams

Kings and queens were probably more dependent on dreams than any other ancient people. Rulers surrounded themselves with priests and soothsayers whose only job was to help make governmental decisions based on dreams. Societies could rise and fall because of these dreams.

In times of crisis, ancient kings would perform religious rituals nightly in order to glean answers to their problems from their dreams. During such times, it was hoped that a god or goddess would appear to the dreamer and give him a very clear message that would require no further interpretation.

One example of this phenomenon occurred around 620 B.C. At that time, Assyrian king Assurbanipal was reluctant

Roman emperor Constantine dreams that an angel holds a cross before him. Ancient rulers made governmental decisions based on their dreams.

to go to war against his enemies, the Elamites. Hoping to find counsel in a dream, Assurbanipal performed magic rituals and went to sleep in the temple of the goddess Ishtar. That night he dreamed that Ishtar appeared before him holding a bow, arrows, and a sword. The goddess told the king she would provide victory for him in battle the next day, and indeed, this dream came true. While skeptics might attribute the king's triumph to coincidence, his decision to go to war because of a dream changed the course of ancient history.

Dreams in the Bible

Like the Assyrians, the Jews of Israel believed that God spoke directly to them—and granted them knowledge and gifts—in dreams. To these ancient people, dreams were a way to see reality more clearly, and the words for *to dream* and *to see* were one in the same.

The Jews believe that the word of God is written in the Old Testament of the Bible, which contains many stories in which God speaks through dreams. For example, when the Hebrew king Solomon was a young boy, according to the Bible, "The Lord appeared to Solomon in a dream by night; and God said 'Ask what I shall give you.'" Solomon asked for wisdom rather than money, power, death to his enemies, or long life. God was pleased and granted Solomon wisdom, a long life, and riches. Since that time, smart people are said to have the "wisdom of Solomon."

Another biblical reference to dreams includes Jacob, who dreamed of a ladder ascending into heaven with angels climbing up and down. As it is written in the Book of Genesis:

> [Jacob] had a dream: a ladder was there, standing on the ground with its top reaching to heaven; and there were angels of God going up it and coming down. And [God] was there, standing over him,

saying, "I am Yahweh, the God of Abraham your father. . . . I will give to you and your descendants the land on which you are lying. Your descendants shall be like the specks of dust on the ground; you shall spread to the west and the east, to the north and the south, and all the tribes of the earth shall bless themselves by you and your descendants. Be sure that I am with you; I will keep you safe wherever you go, and bring you back to this land, for I will not desert you before I have done all that I have promised you."

Jacob's ladder dream has had an influence on culture for thousands of years. It is referenced in countless paintings, plays, songs, and stories and has been used by some to claim that God gave the land of Israel to the Jewish people.

Many references to dreams are found in the Bible. One of the more significant is Jacob's dream of angels climbing a ladder to heaven.

Gabriel, the Prince of Dreams

Dreams also figure prominently in the Talmud, the sixty-three-volume Jewish holy book that combines biblical stories with commentaries by rabbis. In fact, dreams are mentioned 217 times in the book, and the chief angel, Gabriel, is known as the prince of dreams. Dreams featuring Gabriel have helped shape the beliefs of some of the world's major religions.

When Gabriel appears in the New Testament, the Christian Bible, he relates important messages through dreams to Joseph and Mary, the parents of Jesus. In one dream, Gabriel tells Joseph that Mary is pregnant with

Jesus. Joseph has a second dream in which Gabriel appears to warn Joseph that Jesus is in danger and that he and Mary should take the child and escape to Egypt. In a third dream, Gabriel advises Joseph that the danger has passed and it is safe to return to Israel. Dreams that include Gabriel are also an important part of Islam. Muslims believe that the angel appeared to Muhammad, the founder of Islam, in a dream and dictated the first chapter, or sura, of the Koran, the sacred scripture of Islam. Gabriel also accompanied Muhammad in another dream, as described by James R. Lewis in *The Dream Encyclopedia:*

> [Mohammad's] great dream of initiation into the mysteries of the cosmos, known as the *Night Journey*, began when the angel Gabriel appeared to him while he was sleeping. . . . Riding . . . a half-human silver mare, Muhammad arrived in Jerusalem, the center of the world, where he conversed and prayed with Abraham, Moses, and Jesus. Then he passed through seven celestial spheres [of heaven and hell], each infused with its own color, to reach across the ocean of white light and, finally, to approach God.[31]

In the Hadith, a companion book to the Koran, Muhammad is described as lying asleep, sweating and shivering as he receives other sura. After such dreams, Muhammad would awaken and describe these dreams to his disciples and then listen to theirs. These messages make up the foundation of Muslim beliefs and Islam draws other important parts of its doctrine from dreams. One follower of Muhammad's described a dream in which he saw a muezzin, or crier, calling the faithful to daily prayers from a minaret in a mosque. Muhammad then incorporated this *adhan*, or call to prayers, as part of the daily tradition of Islam, which is practiced today by Muslims all over the world.

Dreams of Buddha

Buddhism, the religion widely practiced in India, China, Japan, and elsewhere, is also based on the dramatic dreams surrounding its founder, Buddha, or the Enlightened One.

The most prominent dream in Buddhism is that of Buddha's mother, Maya, who was the queen of a powerful tribe in present-day Nepal. Maya dreamed that she gave birth to Buddha. The dream is described on the Life of Buddha web page:

> Queen Maha Maya was the daughter of King Anjana. . . . Such was her beauty that the name Maya, meaning "vision" was given to her. But it was Maya's virtues and talents that were her most wonderful qualities, for she was endowed with the highest gifts of intelligence and piety. . . .
>
> One full moon night, sleeping in the palace, the queen had a vivid dream. She felt herself being carried away by four devas (spirits) to Lake Anotatta in the Himalayas. After bathing her in the lake, the devas clothed her in heavenly cloths, anointed her with perfumes, and bedecked her with divine flowers. Soon after a white elephant, holding a white lotus flower in its trunk, appeared and went round her three times, entering her womb through her right side. Finally the elephant disappeared and the queen awoke, knowing

Maya's dream, shown here in a stone carving, is prominently featured in Buddhist art.

she had been delivered an important message, as the elephant is a symbol of greatness in Nepal. The next day, early in the morning, the queen told the king about the dream. The king was puzzled and sent for some wise men to discover the meaning of the dream. . . . The wise men said, "Your Majesty, you are very lucky. The devas have chosen our queen as the mother of the Purest-One and the child will become a very great being." The king and queen were very happy when they heard this.[32]

As a cornerstone of Buddhism, Maya's dream has been re-created in thousands of paintings, stone reliefs, and sculptures since it occurred more than forty-five hundred years ago. In addition, Maya's dream has inspired the belief among some Buddhist women that they can become pregnant in dreams. Most important, however, is the dream's significance to the religion that has billions of followers. As Serinity Young writes in *Dreams:* "Here, at the very beginnings of Buddhism, dreaming is central. Indeed, there is the suggestion that without Maya's dream, there would be no Buddha and hence no Buddhism."[33]

Native American Visions and Dreams

Perhaps no culture has been so influenced by dreams as the Native Americans, who used dream visions to govern nearly every aspect of their lives. Dreams were used to determine when to hunt and fish, when to go to war, and when to make peace. In fact, traditionally, Native Americans believe that dreams are the real world, and waking life is an illusion. This concept is explained by Luke Blue Eagle in *Dreaming with the Wheel:*

Native [Americans] used to look at the dream world as the real world. . . . They believed that what we did in the dream world had direct influence over what we would do in the awakened world. They believed that the dream world or the dreamtime had physical consequences, that what you were doing in the dream world was creating what was happening in the physical. They believed that . . . we are all in one big dream that is the Creator's dream, and that's what's creating the world we're in.[34]

Since they believed that dreams were the source of reality, the lives of Native Americans revolved around dreams and dreaming. From the time they were very young, Native Americans attempted to understand the world around them and gain religious knowledge through dreams. Children were encouraged to remember their dreams and speak of them to parents, relatives, and holy men called shamans. The wisdom of the elders helped young people understand their dreams and interpret their meaning in search of good or bad omens. For example, a child might have a dream about a bear. Since bears were respected for their strength and wisdom, its words or actions in the dream were given great importance. If the bear was seen catching fish in its claws in a certain area of a nearby river, tribal elders might send the child to that place to go fishing. If a bear was seen battling a rival tribe, it might mean that the child should build strength and stamina in case of enemy attack.

To help separate good dream messages from bad, some tribes, such as the Lakota, utilized small, circular items called dream catchers, which were made from feathers, stone, leather, and beads. Dream catchers were hung over an individual's bed and were said to separate the positive visions in dreams, which were helpful, from the negative messages, which could steer the dreamer in the wrong direction. Dream catchers are explained on the Native American Dream Catchers web page:

The Dream Catcher is a web, resembling a spider's web, only it has a hole in the center. . . . While you sleep, when a bad dream comes to haunt you, it gets confused by the web and gets caught in it. The stones and trinkets on the web hold that bad dream there until Morning, when the sun shines on it and burns them away. The good Dreams, being more pure and intuitive, easily navigate through the hole in the center, and enter into your Dream time.[35]

Vision Quests

Nightly dreams provided a constant source of knowledge and inspiration to Native American children. By the time young people reached puberty, however, they were anxious to seek out knowledge in a special dream, called a vision quest, that would in some way define their personality. This was a rite of passage for almost all Native American teenagers, and each vision was personal and unique.

Before a vision quest, it was necessary to perform physical and religious rituals, such as praying, staying awake for days, fasting, and taking hallucinogenic drugs. The stress

A Yurok Indian displays a dream catcher. Native Americans believe that dream catchers protect sleepers from bad dreams.

caused by this behavior was thought to help the visionary purify the body, forget trivial matters, and make the mind more receptive to spiritual messages.

When it was time to seek the vision, the young man or woman would spend as long as ten days alone in the wilderness without food. During this time, sleep would be filled with wild, and sometimes terrifying, dreams. Typically, a person having such dreams would see a being who might take many forms—animal, human, or supernatural. The being offered such things as compassion, insight, good fortune, and spiritual guidance. It might instruct the dreamer on choosing life's work, or tell the dreamer to adapt a special diet or manner of dress to increase spiritual power. Individual dreams also might be relevant to the spiritual life of the entire tribe. In such a case, the visionary might become a religious leader in order to teach tribespeople a new religious dance, song, or ritual seen during the vision quest.

After the quest was over, the vision would play an important role throughout the rest of the visionary's life. If the dream was of a specific animal or plant, this would become the totem, or symbolic religious emblem for the dreamer. The visionary believed that he had inherited some of the characteristics of his totem, such as the swiftness of the deer or the sharp eyes of the owl.

Those who dreamed of gods, spirits, or supernatural creatures might be inspired to become healers and shamans. These religious leaders would rely heavily on dreams, sometimes using them to talk to the souls of the dead or to take mystical journeys to the lands of the supreme spirit.

Dreams as Musical Inspiration

People on vision quests sometimes dreamed of songs, which were later taught to others and made part of the tribal tradition. This act of creativity is common to all cultures, according to *Dreams* author Nancy Grace:

[There] exists numerous age-old traditions of seeking spirit songs in dreams and of bringing back sacred melodies and lyrics from the dream world to waking life—for power, for healing, for use in ritual, for community guidance, or for confirmation of a person's calling as a shaman, priest, or teacher. Among the many treasures that have been found in

A Shaman's Dreams

Native American religious leaders, called shamans, depended on dreams to heal the sick and direct the daily lives of tribespeople. In *Apache Life-Way* by Morris Edward Opler, an unnamed shaman explains that he has been guided his entire life by dreams, and that dreams have helped him fight against sickness and danger:

> The dreams always come [unexpectedly], and, whenever there is danger ahead, I dream a warning. Whenever someone is sick, I dream of what plant to use as medicine. In case of danger I [would] see the enemy leader face to face, and he would tell me when the battle was to occur. In sickness I would actually see the plants to use. All my dreams have come true. I consider myself lucky and ascribe my present [old] age to dream help. I have been in many battles, but my dreams have told me what to do, and so I have never been wounded. I tell my close friends about my dreams and help them too. I must be a shaman or I couldn't dream this way.

Shamans use their own dreams to protect and heal their tribes.

the land of dreaming, music most certainly is one of them.[36]

In fact, many composers have received musical inspiration in their dreams. These composers, in turn, wrote melodies and invented forms of music that remain a popular part of society today.

Examples of immortal songs that first appeared in dreams are numerous. The classical composer George Frideric Handel claimed that parts of his famed oratorio *The Messiah*, which is played throughout the Western world around Christmastime, came to him in a dream. Robert Schumann claimed that his colleagues Felix Mendelssohn and Franz Schubert visited him in dreams and presented him with musical themes, which he remembered and recalled once awake.

Richard Wagner is another composer who found dreaming to be productive and creative. When he wrote to a friend about *Tristan und Isolde*, an opera he had recently composed, he said, "For once you are going to hear a dream, I dreamed all this: never could my poor head have invented such a thing purposely."[37]

In more recent times, rocks musicians, from the Beatles' Paul McCartney to Billy Joel and Sting, have credited dreams as the source of their music. In fact, Joel said that all of his songs were inspired by dreams. Sting said, "I think any artist who ignores their dreams is ignoring half of their creative potential."[38]

Words and Pictures

While composers may dream up melodies or words, many well-known authors have used dream imagery to write stories that have strongly influenced culture. Nineteenth-century author Robert Louis Stevenson, who wrote the classic horror story *The Strange Case of Dr. Jekyll and Mr. Hyde*, said that the story was revealed to him in dreams by elflike creatures he called "the Little People" and "Brownies." Unlike other authors who write with the full knowledge of what shape their stories will take, Stevenson said he did not know how *Dr. Jekyll and Mr. Hyde* would end until these dream beings finally told him. As Stevenson writes, the Brownies "do one-half my work for me while I am fast asleep, and in all human likelihood, do the rest for me as well, when I am wide awake and fondly suppose I do it myself."[39]

Another famous horror story, *Frankenstein*, was inspired by a nightmare experienced by its author Mary Shelley. Shelley had a dream in which the story appeared one night in 1816, after she and several authors, including poet Lord Byron, spent the night telling ghost stories. Before bed, Byron challenged each writer to make up a horror story. That night Shelley had a vivid dream in which a hideous corpse sparked to life and stared at her with watery yellow eyes. In her dream, Shelley recalled thinking, "I have found it! What terrified me will terrify the others; and I need only describe the spectre which has haunted my midnight pillow."[40] Since Shelley's dream, the Frankenstein monster has become an icon in modern culture.

Dozens of other well-known authors, including Samuel Taylor Coleridge, Edgar Allan Poe, Rudyard Kipling, H.G. Wells, Jack Kerouac, Franz Kafka, Charlotte Brontë, and Graham Greene, have been inspired by dreams to write stories that have had a major impact on society.

Painters and Filmmakers

Many painters have also been strongly influenced by dreams. In the late nineteenth century, French artist Henri Rousseau painted his dream visions on canvas. His work influenced an entire style of art known as surrealism, which expresses dreamlike pictures by utilizing fantasy images and strange contrasts of subject matter.

Paul McCartney Dreams "Yesterday"

Perhaps the most famous song to appear to its composer in a dream is "Yesterday," written by Paul McCartney and recorded by his band, the Beatles, in 1965. The complete melody for "Yesterday" came to McCartney in a flash of inspiration in a dream. Upon awakening, he sat down at a piano, played the song, and wrote it down. There was a problem, however. Since the song was so clear in his dream, McCartney believed he might have heard it somewhere else and subconsciously plagiarized it. As McCartney says in *Dreams*, edited by Kelly Bulkeley: "I liked the melody a lot but because I dreamed it I couldn't believe I'd written it. I thought, 'No, I've never written like this before.' But I had the tune, which was the magic thing."

For about a month, McCartney could not believe that the dream melody was his, so he played it for other musicians and songwriters and asked them if they ever heard it before. Possibly because he recalled the song in the morning, McCartney gave it the temporary title "Scrambled Eggs." After a month, he said about the song, "If no-one claimed it after a few weeks then I would have it." Eventually, McCartney added the words to "Yesterday," his dream melody, and the song went on to set records. By 2002, the song was played an estimated 6 million times on U.S. radio stations alone. It remains the most covered song ever, having been recorded by more than three thousand artists other than the Beatles.

Paul McCartney dreamed of the melody for the hit song "Yesterday."

One of Rousseau's most famous paintings, *The Dream*, shows a nude woman reclining on a couch, set, incongruously, in an enchanted forest with huge pastel flowers, crouching lions, and a mysterious snake charmer playing the flute. Rousseau said that he dreamed the scene in the painting in which the reclining woman is transported to the forest of her dreams.

In the twentieth century, painters took surrealism to new heights. Salvador Dali, whose often-eerie paintings have come to define surrealism, was strongly inspired by Freud's *The Interpretation of Dreams*. Following Freud's theories about dreams representing repressed thoughts and desires, the painter attempted to create art from the depths of his subconscious. To do so, Dali would purposely fall asleep sitting up uncomfortably in a chair placed in front of a blank canvas. When the artist jerked awake, he would attempt to paint his dream images while they were fresh in his mind. Dali called these works "hand-painted dream photographs."[41]

Filmmakers, like painters, use dreamlike surrealistic images in their work. Some extremely influential directors have relied on their dreams to create their movies. For

An Inventor's Dream

Inventors are often dreamers who hope their creations will improve peoples' lives. Elias Howe, who struggled with a way to make a machine to sew clothing, was one such inventor. Howe's early sewing machines, however, which placed the eye in the middle of the needle, would not work properly. In *All About Dreams*, Gayle Delaney describes how a dream that Howe had in 1846 led to the invention of the modern sewing machine:

One night, [Howe] dreamt that he was captured by a tribe of [warriors] who took him a prisoner before their king. "Elias Howe," roared the monarch, "I command you on pain of death to finish this machine at once."

Cold sweat poured down his brow, his hands shook with fear, his knees quaked. Try as he would, the inventor could not get the missing [part] in the problem over which he had worked so long. All this was so real to him that he cried aloud. In the vision he saw himself surrounded by . . . painted warriors, who formed a hollow square about him and led him to the place of execution. Suddenly he noticed that near the heads of the spears which his guards carried, there were eye-shaped holes! He had solved the secret! What he needed was a needle with an eye near the point! He awoke from his dream, sprang out of bed, and at once made a whittled model of the eye-pointed needle.

Artist Salvador Dali was inspired by Sigmund Freud's dream research. The artist incorporated dream images into many of his paintings.

example, celebrated Swedish director Ingmar Bergman attempted to create scenes from his dreams as accurately as possible in movies such as *Naked Night* and *Wild Strawberries*. Italian director Federico Fellini, who filled his movies with bizarre dreamlike imagery, pointed out the similarities between films and dreams:

> Talking about dreams is like talking about movies, since the cinema uses the language of dreams; years can pass in a second and you can hop from one place to another. It's a language made of image.

And in the real cinema, every object and every light means something, as in a dream.[42]

Fellini's dream-based motion pictures changed the history of filmmaking, influenced millions of filmgoers, and have become part of culture at large. The director, however, was simply following the ancient tradition of storytellers, artists, and musicians, who used dreams as a source of inspiration. The works created by these artists, in turn, inspired others to make new paintings, songs, books, and films. In this way, the power of dreams has played a major role in shaping the world as it is today, and will, no doubt, continue to do so.

Chapter 4

Telepathic Dreaming

At times, throughout history, dreams have acted as windows on the future, a way to gain a fleeting glimpse of the unpredictable events that lay ahead. Called telepathic, premonitory, or precognitive dreams, some people believe that these night visions have predicted future incidents good, bad, commonplace, and cataclysmic. These dreams seem to most often occur one or two days before the actual event.

Premonitory dreams may be broken down into three categories: prophetic dreams, in which future events are revealed or foretold; warning dreams, in which future events are presented in a way that the dreamer may prevent or alter the outcome; and paranormal dreams, in which events unknown to the dreamer are picked up from a person who is awake. Such dreams are particularly mysterious because, while thousands of people have claimed to have had them, scientists cannot explain them—or even prove that they exist.

Striking Lucky?

Whenever there are wars, shipwrecks, mining accidents, or other great catastrophes, dozens of people have come forward to say that they had premonitory dreams about the incident. Skeptics, however, dismiss the validity of such dreams, saying that dreams that predict the future are simply

Many people claim to have dreamed of events before they occur. Scientists are unable to prove that such dreams are possible.

coincidental. They point out that with billions of people on Earth having dozens of dreams every night, a few thousand people are bound to have a dream about disaster every night. As Aristotle writes in *Aristotle on Sleep and Dreams*, since people "have many visions of all kinds, they can be expected to strike lucky now and again."[43]

Those who doubt the existence of precognitive dreams also point out that some people falsely claim to have had precognitive dreams in order to draw attention to themselves. More often, people may reinterpret their past dreams in order to fit in with a recent disaster. For example, people might read a newspaper article about a mining disaster and recall a dream in which they saw someone buried under falling rocks. Although there may be a connection between the dream and reality, it does not mean that the dream foretold the disaster.

To counter the claims of skeptics, researchers who believe in precognitive dreams have compiled some interesting statistics to make their case. In 1886, the Society for

Psychical Research (SPR) analyzed five thousand dreams and discovered that 702, or a little more than 14 percent, were premonitory. In the 1960s, researchers at the Institute of Parapsychology at Duke University studying telepathy in general, found that out of 3,290 precognitive experiences, 68 percent occurred in dreams.

Presidential Premonitions

While a small number of people claim to have telepathic dreams about tragedies that befall others, some dream about their own deaths. These visions are a chilling reminder that, on occasion, nightmares may come true.

One of the most well-documented cases of someone envisioning his own death in a dream occurred in 1865. At that time, President Abraham Lincoln had a prophetic dream in which he was lying in bed in the White House. In the dream, he heard sobbing and got up to walk into the East Room, where he saw a coffin holding a corpse. Lincoln describes the rest of his dream:

> Around [the coffin] were stationed soldiers who were acting as guards; and there was a throng of people, some gazing mournfully upon the corpse, whose face was covered, others weeping pitifully. "Who is dead in the White House?" I demanded of one of the soldiers. "The President," was his answer; "he was killed by an assassin!" Then came a loud burst of grief from the crowd, which awoke me from my dream. I slept no more that night; and although it was only a dream, I have been strangely annoyed by it ever since.[44]

Several weeks later, the scene from Lincoln's dream became reality: The president was shot in the head and killed by John Wilkes Booth on April 14, 1865.

Those who believe that Lincoln was able to witness his funeral before it happened offer theories hoping to explain

A Dream That Changed History

German dictator Adolf Hitler started World War II in 1939 when his Nazi soldiers invaded Poland. In the following years, as many as 100 million Europeans died in that war. During World War I, however, Hitler was simply a corporal fighting in foxholes in France. But as Stuart Holroyd explains in *Dream World*, Corporal Hitler had a telepathic dream that allowed him to escape death—and go on to change the course of history:

A dream that was both prophetic and far-reaching in its effects upon the world was experienced by an Austrian soldier in a battlefield of World War I. One day in 1917, Corporal Adolf Hitler of the Bavarian Infantry awoke suddenly from a dream in which he had been buried beneath an avalanche of earth and molten iron, and had felt blood flowing down his chest. He was actually lying unharmed in his shelter in a trench not far from the French army. All was quiet. Nevertheless, his dream worried him. He left the shelter, stepped over the [low protective barrier around] the trench, and advanced into the no man's land between the armies. A part of his mind told him that he was being stupid, that he was in danger of being hit by a stray bullet or by shrapnel; but he continued like a sleepwalker. A sudden burst of fire, followed by a loud explosion nearby, made him fall to the ground. Corporal Hitler decided that he would be safer in the shelter than in the open country, so he hurried back. But the shelter was no longer there. In its place was an immense crater. Everyone in the shelter and that section of the trench had been instantly buried. The experience nurtured Hitler's conviction that a great destiny awaited him. And had he not acted on his dream premonition, the history of our time would have been entirely different.

Adolf Hitler had a telepathic dream as a corporal during World War I that saved his life.

the phenomenon of premonitory dreams. One complicated premise implies that events that will happen in the future can somehow release energies that can alter the past. For example, when Lincoln was shot, some mysterious force was let loose that was able to travel back in time to warn the president of his untimely demise. Skeptics, however, say that Lincoln's dream might not have been so mysterious—he was constantly receiving death threats as a wartime president during the Civil War. They point out that other presidents, such as James Garfield and William McKinley, who were also assassinated, had premonitions of their own deaths based on real threats from the general public.

Mark Twain once dreamed that his brother, Henry, had died. Several days later, Henry was killed in an explosion.

Dreams of Death

Not many people dream of their own death. Instead, it is more common to dream that a loved one has recently died. Sometimes these nightmares come true. In a case almost as famous as Lincoln's, author Mark Twain had a premonitory dream in the late 1850s concerning his brother Henry Clemens. At the time, Twain, who was twenty-three, was not yet a published author but worked as a pilot on the *Pennsylvania*, a steamboat on the Mississippi River. One night Twain dreamt that Henry, who also worked on the *Pennsylvania*, was lying in a metal coffin balanced between two chairs. A bouquet of white flowers, with a crimson rose in the center, was laying on his chest. Twain awoke from the dream, described the disturbing images to his sister, then forgot about it.

After the dream, Twain was transferred onto another steamboat while Henry stayed aboard the *Pennsylvania*. Several days later, Twain learned that the *Pennsylvania* had blown up, killing 150 people. Twain went to the accident site and found his brother lying in a metal coffin resting on two chairs, exactly as in his dream, but without the flowers. As Twain stood in shock and grief, an elderly nurse approached the coffin and laid a bouquet of white flowers, with a single crimson rose, on Henry's chest.

Twain later wrote about the incident in *Life on the Mississippi*. As a result of the event, he developed a life-long interest in telepathy, which he called "mental telegraphy." Twain described this phenomenon in a letter he wrote to a friend: "Certainly mental telegraphy . . . is always silently at work. . . . I imagine we get most of our thoughts out of somebody else's head . . . and not always out of the heads of acquaintances, but, in the majority of cases, out of the heads of strangers."[45]

Shipwreck Dreams

Telepathic dream researchers offer their own explanations as to how a person who is dying hundreds of miles away can tell a loved one of the tragedy. Using the theory that energies from a soul or spirit are released during catastrophes, it is said that victims are somehow inexplicably able to travel through space in order to appear in someone's dream. As author Jacob Schwartz explains,

> [Dream] telepathy usually occurs when the persons "sending" the message is under great stress, and the receiver of the message is in a relaxed sleep . . .

state. For example, it is fairly common during war or natural disasters, and massive accidents that a sleeping parent or loved one of the victim suddenly awakes startled because of the vivid impression that their child or loved one has been injured, is frightened, or in intensive pain. Battlefield and accident scenes are seen by the loved ones in dreams too.[46]

One of the most well-researched cases of a calamity causing telepathic dreams was the sinking of the luxurious British ocean liner RMS *Titanic* after it hit an iceberg on April 14, 1912. This tragedy, which killed more than fifteen hundred men, women, and children, was envisioned by about twenty people who later stated that they had premonitory dreams—or some would say nightmares— concerning the *Titanic*.

One of the most dramatic cases of premonitions occurred during the final moments of the disaster. Hundreds of miles away from the catastrophe, in New York City, Marianne Gracie heard a command in her dreams that she should get on her knees and pray for those at sea. Gracie awoke and obeyed the command. At the same time, her husband Major Archibald Gracie was sinking in the icy waters after jumping from the *Titanic*. The major, who survived the ordeal by clinging to an overturned lifeboat, later said that while he was drowning he sent a mental message to his wife to tell her he was dying and that they would meet again in heaven. He later said that his message to his wife, and her prayers, allowed him to survive.

While a telepathic message between a husband and wife who think alike after spending years together may be understandable, other premonitory dreams about the *Titanic* were between strangers. Renowned writer Graham Greene, who was only seven when the *Titanic* went down, later wrote about a dream he had exactly at the same time that the ship was sinking:

On the April night of the Titanic disaster . . . I dreamt of a shipwreck. One image of the dream has remained with me for more than sixty years: a man in oilskins [cloth treated with oil to make it waterproof] bent double . . . under the blow of a great wave.[47]

Skeptics who research such claims label them "vague forebodings" and "after the fact claims of prescience."[48] But even these skeptics were unable to explain the uncanny details provided by those, like Greene, who saw the catastrophe only in their dreams.

The Mining Disaster

One of the most studied cases of group premonitions comes from a calamity that occurred on October 21, 1966, in the little mining town of Aberfan, Wales. On that day,

Survivors in lifeboats watch as the Titanic *sinks. Several people reported having premonitory or telepathic dreams about the disaster.*

at 9:15 A.M., the village was buried under an avalanche of half a million tons of coal waste that had been piled on a hill high above the town. The mountain of coal waste, which had been loosened by two days of heavy rain, killed 116 children and twenty-eight adults when it buried an elementary school and other buildings.

After the disaster, reports of premonitory dreams began to fill newspapers. Perhaps the most chilling was reported by the mother of one of the deceased students, Eryl Mai Jones. The night before the disaster, the nine-year-old Eryl told her mother: "I dreamed I went to school and there was no school there. Something black had come down all over it."[49]

Claims of other dreams that predicted the disaster came in from all over Great Britain. A woman in Plymouth, England, known only as Mrs. Milden, dreamed of a little boy with his hair cut in long bangs who was pulled from a coal avalanche by a rescue worker wearing a

Rescue workers rest at the scene of a coal avalanche in Aberfan, Wales. So many people reported premonitory dreams about the disaster that three independent studies were conducted to research the phenomenon.

strange peaked hat. Milden described her dream to six people at church on October 20, 1966, one day before the accident. The night of the accident, as the media covered the rescue efforts on television, a reporter talked to a small boy with bangs who had been rescued by a worker wearing the exact same hat described in the dream.

Similar premonitory dreams of the Aberfan disaster are described by author Preston E. Dennett:

> One lady had a nightmare that she suffocated in "deep blackness." Another dreamed of a small child being buried by a large landslide. Another clearly saw a schoolhouse be buried by an avalanche of coal, and rescue workers digging frantically for survivors. Another woke up from a nightmare in which she was being buried alive.
>
> On the morning of the disaster, [one woman] woke from a dream in which she saw children being overcome by "a black, billowing mass." Probably the clearest of the premonitions was reported by a man in northwestern England who claimed that the night before the disaster, he had a dream which consisted only of letters being spelled out in dazzling light, A-B-E-R-F-A-N. At the time, the dream had no meaning to him. Hours later, he would realize with horror what it meant.[50]

Since so many people reported such dreams, three independent studies were conducted to examine the phenomenon. Final reports concluded that there were at least twenty-four people who had premonitions or precognitive dreams about the disaster. London psychiatrist J.C. Barker, who headed one study, wrote: "The time had surely come to call a halt to attempts to prove or disprove precognition. We should instead set about trying to harness and utilize it with a view to preventing further disasters."[51]

Registering Premonitions

Barker was so impressed with the study's findings that, in 1967, he founded the British Premonitions Bureau. The purpose of this bureau was to create official records of premonitory dreams that would, theoretically, serve as an early warning system and avert some of the disasters that might happen.

During the six years that the bureau was in existence, it received 1,206 calls. Of these calls, several were uncannily accurate, according to the Central Premonitions Registry website:

> Some of [the dreams] indeed seem[ed] truly precognitive of events of public interest, such as the death of 14 children in a fire in an institute for the [mentally disabled], or the death of a pair of twins that were trapped in a refrigerator and suffocated. But there was no clear pattern, and there was never a flood of reports that all referred to the same incident. . . . [Altogether] there were many fewer significant cases than expected.[52]

Other problems existed with dreams recorded with the British Premonitions Bureau. Of those who foresaw disaster in their dreams, most were unable to accurately pinpoint dates or times. In addition, most of the predictions came from only a small number of people, whom Barker called "human seismographs," after machines used to measure earthquakes. With only a few significant cases to report, the bureau closed down.

Meanwhile, in 1968, on the other side of the Atlantic, the Central Premonitions Registry was founded in New York City. This group, based on the British Premonitions Bureau, divided the material it received into eleven categories, such as death, disaster, news, famous people, natural disasters, war, space, and politics. After the assassination of

After the deaths of President John F. Kennedy (pictured) and his brother, Robert, the Central Premonitions Registry created a category for reports of dreams about the Kennedy family.

President John F. Kennedy in 1963, and his brother Robert in 1968, the group created a special category for premonitory dreams about the Kennedy family.

The Central Premonitions Registry recorded several successful premonitions, such as one woman's dream in 1968 that predicted that the United States would be attacked by a foreign country somewhere in Southern California. As unlikely as this seemed at the time, a few days later, a Mexican navy ship fired on an American fishing vessel in San Diego in a dispute over fishing rights in nearby Mexican waters.

In another premonitory vision, someone dreamed that astronauts aboard the *Apollo* spacecraft, which was circling the earth at the time, were sick and would have difficulty landing. Several days later, the capsule landed upside down during a rough landing in the Pacific, and the crew was suffering from colds.

Although the registry could point to a few such successful dreams, it closed down after several years due to lack of funds. In the mid-1990s, however, the Central Premonitions Registry set up a website where people could submit any premonitory dreams that they might have had. But, as the registry admits, predicting the future in dreams—and then doing something about it— is a difficult task:

> The main problem [is] that most precognitive dreams concern personal and trivial matters, and

even when they refer to a public event, they are usually from that person's subjective perspective. Also, since most precognitive dreams are fulfilled within a few hours, usually people don't have time to report them until it's too late. So this is why it's hard to use [the registry] for practically averting disasters, and this is why you should e-mail us the dream immediately upon writing it down.[53]

Communicating in Dreams

In the 1960s, while some were attempting to register premonitory dreams, researchers Montague Ullman and Stanley Krippner conducted a series of experiments attempting to scientifically prove their existence. In their research, between 1962 and 1972, they tried to prove that people who were awake could telepathically communicate with sleepers—and even influence their dreams.

The experiments, conducted at the Maimonides Medical Center in Brooklyn, are known as the Maimonides Project on Paranormal Dreams. During tests, an awake subject stared at a picture of a well-known painting by a famous artist and "sent" it mentally to a sleeper. The paintings portrayed vivid colors and subjects such as dancing women, lions, wine bottles, or coffins that could evoke strong dream imagery. Some images were sent to sleepers from a room thirty-two feet away, others from a distance of fourteen miles.

After the images were sent, the dreamers were gently awakened and asked to tape-record their dreams. This was repeated up to five times per night. In the morning, the subjects were asked again about their dreams. The results showed that some people were able to describe at least some of the images sent to them telepathically; several subjects seemed astonishingly telepathic at either sending or receiving messages. One man was able to correctly identify

A Chilling Nightmare on Ice

Since people who have dangerous jobs often face real hazards, it is not unusual for them to have disaster dreams. The Premonitions of Disaster web page relates one nightmare that came true. It was dreamed by a seal hunter who worked on frigid icebergs:

In 1914, one hundred twenty Newfoundland sealers were abandoned on an [iceberg] in the north Atlantic ocean during winter. Due to the incompetence of the ship's captain and others, the missing men were not noticed for two days and two nights. By the time they were rescued more than half were dead. It was the worst disaster to strike the Newfoundland sealing community in many years.

However, the disaster did not come without warning. One of the 55 survivors later told of a dream he had two weeks before the disaster. According to [a] report on the disaster: "John Howlet had suffered a chilling nightmare weeks before. In his dream he was on a mountain of ice, lost and freezing. He was alone, terribly and frighteningly alone, but everywhere he wandered there were vague, indefinable 'things' on the ice around him—things with no particular shape that he could make out. He found himself walking among those things, unable to find his way, wondering what they were and dreading them. In his dream he was counting, counting, counting. . . . He was still counting the white mounds when he awoke, shivering and terribly depressed."

Unfortunately, the dream was not enough for him to stop from joining the crew of the ship, *Newfoundland*, most of whom would be dead in a matter of days. And only afterwards was he to recognize the white mounds for what they were—bodies covered with snow.

Seal hunters drag furs across the ice in Newfoundland. People with dangerous jobs often have disaster dreams.

images in six paintings mentally sent to him over the course of eight nights. Ullman calculated that the odds against this happening by accident were 1,000 to 1.

In another experiment, a man tried to predict the future by dreaming of a previously selected picture that he would be shown by researchers the following night. Remarkably, this man, who was known for his telepathic powers, was able to correctly guess the painting on seven out of eight nights. Again, the odds against this were calculated at 1,000 to 1.

In 1972, Ullman discontinued his experiments. But during the decade studying telepathy in a clinical setting, he reached the conclusion that some people are more capable of telepathic and premonitory dreams than others. Skeptics, however, believe that Ullman and his fellow researchers ignored people whose dreams did not seem telepathic, only using those dreams that seemed to back their theories. In addition, images dreamed by test subjects were so common that they could typically be found in many classical paintings and even billboards and television commercials. Despite the skepticism from critics, Ullman came to believe that telepathic dreams are a very real phenomenon. He is joined by dozens of researchers who do believe that, for some mysterious reason, some dreamers—on some nights—are able to see into the future and communicate with people who are awake.

Chapter 5

Dream Power

Over the centuries it has been said that dreams have great powers that go beyond scientific and physical boundaries. As far back as the eleventh century, Tibetan holy men were using mental and physical rituals, called dream yoga, in order to help practitioners achieve spiritual enlightenment, a blessed state marked by the absence of desire or suffering. In modern times, people continue to practice dream yoga and also use methods based on this ancient practice to solve problems, heal sickness and disease, cure addictions, and even fly through space.

Those who find such power in dreams have developed techniques, such as keeping dream journals and undergoing intensive dream analysis, in attempts to understand what their dreams are trying to tell them. While skeptics doubt that dreams have the amazing powers some attribute to them, dozens of books are published every year that claim people can harness dream power in order to find love, enhance creativity, relieve stress, lose weight, obtain riches, and even talk to dead relatives. As scientists try to explain such phenomena, or prove they even exist, thousands of people are reading books and attending classes and seminars in attempts to harness the supernatural powers of their dreams.

Recalling Dreams

Dream researchers say that the first step toward utilizing dream power is to remember dreams as clearly as possible upon awakening so that they may be analyzed at a later time.

Dreams are recalled in their most vivid detail immediately after the REM sleep period ends. Only five minutes after the dream is finished, memories of it begin to fade. After ten minutes, the dream is often completely forgotten. Those who wish to capture the clearest memories set alarm clocks to awaken them every ninety minutes throughout the night. This drastic method is imperfect, however, since it may interrupt dreams and disrupt sleep. Those who wish to sidestep this problem train themselves to awaken after each dream by concentrating on the desire to do so before bedtime. By practicing this technique over time, the idea of awakening and remembering dreams becomes part of the

Researchers say that the first step toward harnessing the power of dreams is to remember them in detail upon waking.

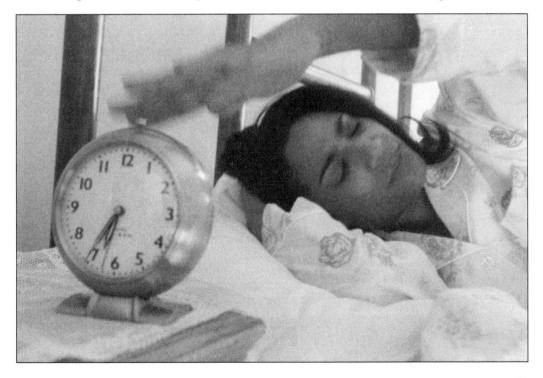

subconscious mind like any other habit. As Patricia Garfield writes in *Creative Dreaming*, "Recording dreams after [self-awakening] from a REM [sleep] will give the most complete and accurate dream recall."[54]

Dream researchers say that another important part of remembering dreams is to write them down immediately upon awakening. This practice, in use since ancient times, allows the dreamer to record the dream images, feelings, or impressions while they are still fresh in the mind. People use pencils and paper, audio tapes, or even drawings, sketches, and pictures for this purpose. During the course of recording the dream, more details often come to light. As dream researcher Craig Webb states: "You'll be surprised at how much more you can remember as you write, speak, draw, paint, etc."[55]

Some people assist their memories by giving each dream a descriptive title. For example, a dream about walking down a long, empty hallway might be called "Visiting an Abandoned House." By remembering the title later, sleep researchers believe the dream is easier to recall.

While some only record dreams that seem very significant, dream researchers believe that even silly or irrelevant dreams may have important meanings that might come to light at a later date. As Garfield writes:

> The dream you dismiss as ridiculous or trivial . . . may be the very one with great potential to blossom beautifully when it's more developed. . . . You will be amazed to find, after you keep a dream diary for a few months, that seemingly unimportant symbols appear again and again. They change in shape and size but are clearly recognizable when written down. They literally grow. You can trace their development over time. . . . Attend patiently to all your dreams and they will provide you with remarkable insights about yourself.[56]

Problem Solving in Dreams

By keeping a dream journal, and rereading it before bed, researchers say that dreams can be analyzed and used to improve life in a number of ways. This includes solving practical problems at school, work, and home. In *Dreams and Destinies*, Beryl Beare explains why some believe dreams have such powers:

> In our dreams we are, in a sense, talking to ourselves. The conversations we have, however, are more meaningful than the rather trivial "thought-talk" . . . [we have] while carrying out boring tasks. When we dream it is our unconscious doing the talking, and listening to it could be more beneficial than we realize. . . .
>
> It is not uncommon for problems to be resolved . . . while we sleep. Some part of the mind seems to continue working on the problem during the night, and in the morning we may find that we have a solution. Occasionally, the answer to a problem comes through a dream.[57]

In order to glean the most problem-solving powers from dreams, people try to direct their dreams. This process, called dream incubation, calls for a person to focus intently on a particular problem before falling asleep in hopes that an answer will be revealed in dreams.

While some believe that dreams are random, subconscious events that cannot be controlled, dream incubation has been shown to be effective in several experiments. In the mid-1970s, Robert Davé conducted experiments in dream incubation with test subjects at Michigan State University. The subjects were hypnotized before sleep and told to dream of a solution to a particular academic, vocational, or personal problem that they were having trouble with in their daily life. Of the group, 75 percent claimed that they were able to solve their problems by analyzing symbols that appeared in their dreams.

Another experiment, led by Deidre Barrett at Harvard Medical School, was conducted by a group of students. Barrett instructed the students to think for fifteen minutes before bedtime about a problem that troubled them at school, work, or with a relationship. In the morning, they were asked to write down their dreams as accurately as possible. On the Incubating Dreams Solves Problems web page, Dr. Henry Reed writes about the results of the experiment:

Memories of dreams begin to fade only five minutes after the dream is over. Writing down dreams immediately upon waking can help people to analyze their dreams later.

One week later, approximately half the students had recalled a dream related to their chosen problem. More than a third of the students believed their dream had solved the problem. Students were more likely to solve a problem of intense personal interest, or a medical problem, than one of a general or academic nature.[58]

Dreaming Students Solve a Problem

Dr. William C. Dement believes that people can sometimes discover the answers to problems while dreaming. In *The Promise of Sleep*, Dement describes a simple problem-solving experiment he conducts with his students at Stanford University:

Let me describe one of my favorite exercises. On three consecutive days, I gave a class of 500 students a problem that required a little creativity. This is one of the problems:

What are the next two letters in this sequence?

O, T, T, F, F

I instructed the students to think about the problem for 15 minutes before bed and to record their dreams upon awakening. Over the three days of the experiment, we got 1,148 responses from 500 students. We found that 87 responses were related to a dream, and if a solution appeared in a dream, we scored it as either correct or incorrect. The correct answer showed up in dreams 9 times. . . . Here is one of the "solution dreams" by a student:

I was standing in an art gallery looking at the paintings on the wall. As I walked down the hall, I began to count the paintings, one, two, three, four, five. But as I came to the sixth and seventh, the paintings had been ripped from their frames! I stared at the empty frames with a peculiar feeling that some mystery was about to be solved. Suddenly I realized that the sixth and seventh spaces were the solution to the problem!

In other words, the sequence O, T, T, F, F, consists of the letters beginning the words one, two, three, four, five, so the next two letters would be S and S, for six and seven.

Seven out of 1,148 is a low percentage, less than 1 percent. But . . . I believe that if people spend a great deal of time thinking about a problem . . . the percentage of their dreams carrying a solution will be much greater than in my classroom experiment.

Sleep experts are unsure as to why a person who cannot solve a problem while awake can solve it while asleep. Some believe this happens because the dreaming brain often mixes illogical and contradictory elements; thinking of unorthodox or unlikely solutions is often a hallmark of problem solving. As William C. Dement writes:

It is a source of endless speculation why the same brain . . . can sometimes see so clearly while dreaming. I think the answer lies in the dreaming brain's ability to ignore many of the norms we live by and to create the unexpected. [In dreams we might] walk out of our own bedroom and into the Oval Office, and it doesn't seem surprising at all. . . . Dreams open us up to possibilities that we would never think of in daily life.

Dreams are also very good at melding paradoxical elements, an essential element of the creative process. Paradoxical combinations are simply grist for the nightly dream mill. . . . [In] waking life we are often blind to combinations of elements that seem paradoxical.[59]

Dreams of Sickness and Healing

While the dreaming brain might be able to analyze complicated problems, some claim it can also be used to cure sickness and disease. According to the Dream Therapy web page, dreams can "warn of oncoming health problems, help diagnose them, suggest treatment, accelerate the healing process, and contribute to life-long health."[60] The belief, while controversial, is nothing new—it was widely promoted by the ancient Egyptians, Greeks, and others.

In modern times, many people have reported that their dreams have healed them or prevented them from becoming sick. This often occurs when a person dreams of a doctor or a nurse. In such a case, the dreamer might actually be receiving medical advice.

Although there is little scientific proof to back claims of dream healing, several researchers have studied this largely uncharted field. For example, Dr. Bernard Siegel, a cancer surgeon and professor at the Yale School of Medicine, has recorded several cases of patients diagnosing their cancer in their dreams. Siegel says a patient "with breast cancer reported [a] dream in which her head was shaved and the word cancer [was] written on it. She awakened with the knowledge that she had brain [cancer]. No physical signs or symptoms were evident until three weeks had passed and [the] diagnosis was confirmed."[61]

Siegel himself had a diagnostic dream, albeit one that was more positive. At one time, the doctor experienced several symptoms of cancer. One night as he lay dreaming, he saw himself in a large group of people, all of whom had cancer. Someone pointed to the doctor and said he did not have the disease. As Siegel writes, "I awoke with the knowledge that I did not have cancer. This was later verified by tests."[62] Diagnosing sickness in dreams may be attributed to the dreamer subconsciously evaluating the health of his or her body.

Some people claim dreaming of a doctor has cured them of a medical problem or prevented them from getting sick.

Visualizing Health

In addition to diagnosing, there are those who claim that they have been cured of cancer and other diseases using dream techniques. Dr. Carl Simonton has developed a program that combines dream power and relaxation to help cancer patients. In one experiment, Simonton treated a sixty-one-year-old man who had throat cancer, which left him about a 10 percent chance of survival. Before bed, the doctor told him to imagine his cancerous tumor bombarded by healing particles of radiation while white blood cells took away the cancer. The man often dreamed of these images and, after seven weeks, discovered that his tumor was shrinking.

Skeptics point out that such events might simply be coincidence and that dream therapies are as yet unproven. The Lucidity Institute, however, offers an explanation of such mysterious cures:

The effects of visual imagery on the body are well-established. . . . [And] healing dream imagery may improve physical health. Medical patients have often used soothing and positive imagery to alleviate pain, and the dream world offers the most vivid form of imagery. Thus, some people have used lucid dreams in overcoming phobias, working with grief, decreasing social . . . anxieties, achieving greater self-confidence and by directing the body image in the dream to facilitate physical healing. The applications . . . deserve clinical study, as they may be the greatest boon that . . . dreaming has to offer.[63]

Dream power may have positive effects on the sick, but even those who advocate such techniques say that they are not a substitute for medical treatments. Instead, they are meant to be used in addition to medical care in order to alleviate pain and suffering.

Treating Addiction

In addition to healing disease, some believe that dreams can be used to help those recovering from addictions. Dement, who once smoked two packs of cigarettes a day, describes a dream that helped him end his addiction to tobacco immediately after he dreamed it:

Like many heavy smokers, I had developed a chronic cough, known as a smoker's hack. One day in 1964 I was coughing into a handkerchief and noticed with a chill that the little flecks of sputum on the white cloth were reddish pink. . . . I sought out a radiologist friend and asked him to order a chest X ray. The next day I went back to his office, full of dread. I will never forget the grim expression on his face as he motioned me to the light box behind his desk. Without a word, he turned and clipped my chest film onto it. Immediately I saw that my lungs harbored a dozen white spots—cancer. The wave of anguish and despair that I felt was overpowering. I could barely breathe. My life was over. I wouldn't see my children grow up. All because I hadn't stopped smoking, even though I knew all about smoking and cancer. "You utter fool," I thought. "You've destroyed your own life!" And then I woke up.

The bloody sputum, the X rays, and the cancer had been a dream—an incredibly vivid and real dream. What a relief. I was reborn.[64]

Research has shown that people can utilize dreams in such a manner to help stop an addiction.

Tibetan Dream Yoga

While dream power has helped people solve practical matters, such as tobacco addiction, it has also been used by practitioners of Tibetan dream yoga who want to change their lives through spiritual enlightenment. Tibetan dream yoga is a practice in which people use intensive dream analysis and meditation to enter a state of sleep, but keep their minds fully conscious. In this condition, they can control the content of their dreams and clearly remember their dream experiences when they awaken. According to Patricia Garfield in *Creative Dreaming:* "This is an astonishing and almost incredible claim to [most people who] . . . find it difficult enough to believe that a dreamer can *become* conscious in a dream . . . to say nothing of *maintaining* unbroken consciousness between sleeping and waking."[65]

Those who practice dream yoga, however, believe that there is no difference between reality and dreams. They believe that this allows them to gain control of their dreams and manipulate them in order to have mystical

People who practice Tibetan dream yoga say they can control their dreams to do such fantastic things as travel through time or have out-of-body experiences.

experiences. To do this, practitioners of dream yoga perform rituals both day and night. While awake, they must continually keep in mind that there is no difference between the waking world and the dream world. As Gyatrul Rinpoche writes in *Ancient Wisdom*, "Throughout the different experiences during the daytime reality, you just keep on . . . [thinking] 'This is a dream, this is a dream, I'm asleep and I'm dreaming,' and this will create a habit."[66]

At night, in addition to other rituals, practitioners of dream yoga chant a prayer, saying: "Tonight may I dream many dreams. May I have many dreams, and may my dreams be very clear. May they be very good. May I recognize the dream as a dream. Simply put, may I apprehend my dream."[67] After taking control, or apprehending, their dream, practitioners say they can explore past lives, speak with mysterious spirits, travel through time, or even have an out-of-body experience, known as astral travel.

On a more practical level, dream yoga is said to help people rid their minds of negative afflictions, which, according to Rinpoche, consist of "desire, hatred, jealousy, pride, and ignorance."[68] The experiences during dream yoga are also said to put the problems of day-to-day life in perspective. According to Alice Ouzounian on the Tibetan Dream Yoga web page, the power of dream yoga can help "free the mind. Release . . . tension and stress. Loosen [bad] habits. . . . Unleash and mobilize creativity. . . . Clarify and dispel confusion. . . . Solve problems. . . . Heal and relax. . . . Unlock aspirations and potentials. . . . Provide spiritual blessings, visions, and guidance."[69]

Astral Travel in Dreams

One of the most mysterious phenomenon associated with dream yoga is the out-of-body experience (OBE), or astral travel. Those who practice this activity believe that within each person there exists another body, known as the astral body, that can travel throughout the world by itself as the "real" body stays behind.

According to studies by the Lucidity Institute, about 20 percent of people have experienced astral travel at least one time. This may be either a frightening experience, described by some as hell, or an enjoyable experience, similar to paradise. As dream researchers Lynne Levitan and Stephen LaBerge state, "OBEs are highly arousing; they can be either deeply disturbing or profoundly moving."[70]

Those experiencing an OBE see a world that is similar to the one they inhabit while awake. During this event, people often experience a surging sense of energy. Odd sounds, such as a humming, a hissing, or a roaring in the ears, can accompany the OBE. Sometimes, however, astral travelers also hear beautiful music during an OBE, as described by Grace Russell in *NAD: A Study of Some Unusual "Other-World" Experiences*, by D. Scott Rogo:

An Out-of-Body Experience

Astral projection is an unexplained phenomenon that happens when people feel that they have left their bodies in order to travel through time and space. In *The Study and Practice of Astral Projection* by Robert Crookall, astral traveler George Hepworth describes such an event that he experienced as he slept:

I seemed to step out of my body and stand beside it, looking down upon it. I felt as light as air. . . . I moved away from my Physical Body towards the door, and to my surprise, I found that the door was no obstruction whatsoever: I simply passed through it. . . .

Just then the thought of my lost love [Margaret] came into my mind. An intense desire to see her seized me . . . and I flew with incredible speed through the darkness. The camp, the lake, the mountains were lost to view almost instantly, while other mountains and lakes came within range of my astonished vision. . . . But I became so confused while journeying that I hardly noticed the landscape that lay far below me. . . . The next moment I was in the room. . . . Margaret was sitting at the bedside of [her sick husband] . . . Edward, with her back toward me. . . . I

strode across the room . . . and called out, "Margaret! Margaret!" For an instant I thought she heard me, for she raised her head as though in the act of listening. . . . I suffered tortures in the thought that I was invisible and could not make her recognize me. . . . I went to her side and placed my hand on hers, hoping that she would feel me near. Perhaps she did. At any rate, she looked up, then rose from her chair, went to the other side of the room, and stood there looking at an old photograph of me.

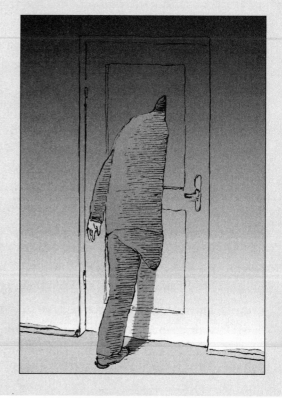

People pass through doors and other objects effortlessly in their dreams in a phenomenon known as astral projection.

[After I left my body] there was music, wonderful music, coming in through the only open window in the room. . . . I felt spellbound. . . . *A very large group of instruments was being played in a way I had never heard music played before. . . . I heard a deep roaring sound, something like the ocean's roar.* This music was of an intensity most unusual. It had meaning and great beauty.[71]

Researchers believe that an OBE such as Russell's might be a specific kind of lucid dream, because it only happens during REM-stage sleep. But people who have such experiences say that they seem much more real than dreams. Unlike lucid dreams, in which a person is conscious that he is dreaming, during OBEs people feel as if they are not dreaming but wide awake.

Some people believe that there is great power in OBEs and that their astral body can accomplish many tasks. These include traveling throughout the world, checking up on relatives thousands of miles away, or even spying on the neighbors. Astral travelers claim they can also communicate with other "out-of-body" people as they journey through the night. Whether or not OBEs are simply vivid dreams or actual physical events has not been answered by science.

Dream Workshops

To learn to astral travel and harness other dream powers, people may take classes or join "dream workshops," where they can gather with others. These classes teach subjects such as spiritual dreaming, dream incubation, healing dreams, out-of-body dreams, and more.

Most dream workshops are led by experienced "dream workers" who guide the group, ask pertinent questions, and encourage speakers if they falter. These workshops are similar to group therapy sessions, where people talk freely about their own dreams and listen to those of others. As Gayle Delaney writes in *All About Dreams:* "If you are fortunate enough to work in a good dream group for six months to a few years, you will learn much about dreams . . . and about human nature. Hearing people's dreams over time show you their real insides."[72]

Not all groups are led by professionals, however, and some dream workshops are simply group discussion ses-

People can learn more about dreams and their significance by attending dream workshops.

sions attended by like-minded people. Those who want to learn how to lead such workshops can buy instructional videos and books on the topic. Others visit Internet chat rooms, newsgroups, and websites dedicated to dream discussion and analysis.

The Gifts of Dreams

Skeptics criticize those who attempt to profit from something as enigmatic as dream power. But there is no shortage of people who are willing to support those who can teach them how their dreams can lead them to a better, more productive, and healthier life. As long as this is so, researchers will continue to work in sleep laboratories while attempting to pin down specific ways that dreams can influence reality. Whether dream power is fact or fantasy, it seems to have had a positive influence on those who try to utilize it. As Garfield writes:

> Your dream life can provide you with many marvelous gifts: creative products, delightful adventures, increased skill in coping with waking life, and a personal laboratory to develop any project of your choice. The party is held several times each night. You are the guest of honor. All you need to do is attend, enjoy, pick up your presents, and return to waking life. . . . You can develop almost total recall for your nightly dream parties and become able to record and use your gifts in waking life.[73]

Notes

Introduction: "What We Do in Our Dreams"

1. Quoted in *Columbia World of Quotations*, s.v. "Nietzsche, Friedrich."

Chapter 1: Dream Science

2. William C. Dement, *The Promise of Sleep*, New York: Dell, 1999, p. 21.
3. Stuart Holroyd, *Dream Worlds*, Garden City, NY: Doubleday, 1976, p. 88.
4. Sandra Shulman, *Nightmares*, New York: Macmillan, 1979 p. 29.
5. Holroyd, *Dream Worlds*, p. 80.
6. Dement, *The Promise of Sleep*, p. 325.
7. Quoted in James R. Lewis, *The Dream Encyclopedia*, Detroit: Visible Ink Press, 1995, pp. 151–52.
8. Quoted in Robert Todd Carroll, "Lucid Dreaming," The Skeptics Dictionary, 2002. www.skepdic.com.
9. Robert Van de Castle, *Our Dreaming Mind*, New York: Ballantine Books, 1994, pp. 275–76.
10. J. Allan Hobson, *The Dreaming Brain*, New York: Basic Books, 1988, p. 296
11. Van de Castle, *Our Dreaming Mind*, pp. 349–50.
12. John E. Mack, *Nightmares and Human Conflict*, Boston: Little, Brown, 1970, p. 13.
13. Hobson, *The Dreaming Brain*, p. 297.

Chapter 2: Interpreting Dreams

14. Quoted in Naphtali Lewis, ed., *The Interpretation of Dreams and Portents*. Toronto: Hakkert, 1976, p. 17.
15. Quoted in Lewis, *The Interpretation of Dreams and Portents*, p. 18.
16. Quoted in Anita Stratos, "Perchance to Dream," Tour Egypt. www.touregypt.net.
17. Quoted in Van de Castle, *Our Dreaming Mind*, p. 55.
18. Artemidorus, *The Interpretation of Dreams*, trans. Robert White. Park Ridge, NJ: Noyes Press, 1975, p. 30.
19. Artemidorus, *The Interpretation of Dreams*, p. 51.
20. Artemidorus, *The Interpretation of Dreams*, p. 90.
21. Artemidorus, *The Interpretation of Dreams*, p. 126.
22. Artemidorus, *The Interpretation of Dreams*, p. 231.
23. Quoted in Van de Castle, *Our Dreaming Mind*, p. 66.
24. Shulman, *Nightmares*, p. 10.
25. Quoted in Van de Castle, *Our Dreaming Mind*, pp. 88–89.
26. Quoted in *Columbia World of Quotations*, s.v. "Freud, Sigmund."
27. Sigmund Freud, *The Interpretation of Dreams*, trans. A.A. Brill. New York: Modern Library, 1994, p. 34.

28. Freud, *The Interpretation of Dream*, pp. 275–76.
29. Robert Todd Carroll, "Psychoanalysis and Sigmund Freud," The Skeptic's Dictionary, 2002. www.skepdic.com.
30. Quoted in Lewis, *The Interpretation of Dreams and Portents*, p. 157.

Chapter 3: Dreams That Inspire

31. Lewis, *The Dream Encyclopedia*, pp. 131–32.
32. BuddhaNet, "Life of Buddha: (Part One) Queen Maya's Dream," 2003. www.buddhanet.net.
33. Quoted in Kelly Bulkeley, ed., *Dreams*. New York: Pulgrave, 2001, p. 10.
34. Quoted in Sun Bear, Wabun Wind, and Shawnodese, *Dreaming with the Wheel*. New York: Simon & Schuster, 1994, p. 33.
35. "Native American Dream Catchers," Native American Dreams, 2003. http://groups.msn.com.
36. Quoted in Bulkeley, *Dreams*, p. 168.
37. Quoted in Van de Castle, *Our Dreaming Mind*, p. 14.
38. Quoted in Bulkeley, *Dreams*, p. 167.
39. Quoted in A. Alvarez, *Night: Night Life, Night Language, Sleep, and Dreams*. New York: W.W. Norton, 1995, p. 200.
40. Quoted in Van de Castle, *Our Dreaming Mind*, p. 16.
41. Quoted in Van de Castle, *Our Dreaming Mind*, p. 11.
42. Quoted in *Columbia World of Quotations*, s.v. "Fellini, Federico."

Chapter 4: Telepathic Dreaming

43. Quoted in David Gallup, *Aristotle on Sleep and Dreams*. Warminster, UK: Aris & Phillips, 1996, p. 111.
44. Quoted in Joe Nickell, "Paranormal Lincoln," Lincoln and the Paranormal: Investigative Files, May/June 1999. www.csicop.org.
45. Quoted in Martin Ebon, "Mark Twain's 'Mental Telegraphy,'" New Paradigm Books, 2001. www.newpara.com.
46. Jacob Schwartz, "Can Dreams Preview the Future," The New Age Directory. www.newage-directory.com.
47. Quoted in Craig Hamilton-Parker, "Titanic Coincidences," www.spiritualists.org.
48. Quoted in Preston E. Dennett, "Premonitions of Disaster," *Atlantis Rising Magazine*. www.atlantisrising.com.
49. Quoted in Holroyd, *Dream Worlds*, pp. 112–13.
50. Dennett, "Premonitions of Disaster."
51. Quoted in Dennett, "Premonitions of Disaster."
52. Central Premonitions Registry, 1995. http://mainportals.com.
53. Central Premonitions Registry.

Chapter 5: Dream Power

54. Patricia Garfield, *Creative Dreaming*. New York: Ballantine Books, 1974, p. 190.
55. Craig Webb, "Harvesting Dreamland," The Dream Foundation, www.dreams.ca.
56. Garfield, *Creative Dreaming*, p. 172.

57. Beryl Beare, *Dreams and Destinies.* North Dighton, MA: JG Press, 1995, pp. 33–34.

58. Henry Reed, "Incubating Dreams Solves Problems," Intuitive-Connections Network, February 17, 2003. www.intuitive-connections.net.

59. Dement, *The Promise of Sleep*, p. 320.

60. "Dream Therapy," NursingPower.net. www.reikinurse.com.

61. Quoted in Gayle Delaney, *All About Dreams.* San Francisco: HarperSanFrancisco, 1998, p. 247.

62. Quoted in Delaney, *All About Dreams*, p. 248.

63. Lucidity Insitute, "Lucid Dreaming FAQ," January 16, 2003. www.lucidity.com.

64. Dement, *The Promise of Sleep*, pp. 292–93.

65. Garfield, *Creative Dreaming*, p. 151.

66. Gyatrul Rinpoche, *Ancient Wisdom.* Ithaca, NY: Snow Lion Publications, 1993, p. 104.

67. Quoted in Rinpoche, *Ancient Wisdom*, p. 105.

68. Rinpoche, *Ancient Wisdom*, p. 95.

69. Alice Ouzounian, "Tibetan Dream Yoga," Hermetic Philosophy and the Mystery of Being, December 30, 2002. www.plotinus.com.

70. Lynne Levitan and Stephen LaBerge, "Out-of-Body Experiences and Lucid Dreams," Lucidity Institute, March 1991. www.lucidity.com.

71. Quoted in D. Scott Rogo, *NAD: A Study of Some Unusual "Other-World" Experiences.* New Hyde Park, NY: University Books, 1970, pp. 38–39.

72. Delaney, *All About Dreams*, p. 259.

73. Garfield, *Creative Dreaming*, p. 172.

For Further Reading

M.J. Abadie, *Teen Dream Power: Unlock the Meaning of Your Dreams.* Rochester, VT: Inner Traditions, 2003. Written by a New Age author who specializes in dream interpretation.

John Bierhorst, ed., *On the Road of Stars: Native American Night Poems and Sleep Charms.* New York: Macmillan, 1994. A collection of Native American poems, sleep charms, and other special night songs intended to soothe, heal, bring on dreams, and aid sleep.

Patricia L. Garfield, *The Dream Book: A Young Person's Guide to Understanding Dreams.* Toronto: Tundra Books, 2002. A book by a psychologist that presents dream scenarios and their meanings, along with ways to solve personal problems through dream analysis.

Andrew T. McPhee, *Sleep and Dreams.* New York: Franklin Watts, 2001. Discusses the nature of sleep and dreams, the causes of and treatments for sleep disorders, and the possible meaning of common dreams.

Lady Stearn Robinson and Tom Gorbett, *The Dreamer's Dictionary: From A to Z: 3,000 Magical Mirrors to Reveal the Meaning of Your Dreams.* London: BT Bound, 1999. An easy-to-use guide with more than 1 million copies in print. Explains how to distinguish four types of dreams, identify dream symbols, and understand meanings.

Tucker Shaw, *Dreams: Explore the You That You Can't Control.* New York: Penguin, 2000. This book emphasizes that dreams are usually not unexplainable symbols, but rather reflect what is going on in a dreamer's mind.

Works Consulted

Books

A. Alvarez, *Night: Night Life, Night Language, Sleep, and Dreams.* New York: W.W. Norton, 1995. A combination of personal observations, scientific research, and literary references concerning the subjects of sleep and dreams.

Artemidorus, *The Interpretation of Dreams.* Trans. Robert White. Park Ridge, NJ: Noyes Press, 1975. An in-depth study of dream symbolism written in the second century B.C. and based on ancient Egyptian dream books.

Sun Bear, Wabun Wind, and Shawnodese, *Dreaming with the Wheel.* New York: Simon & Schuster, 1994. A book that educates readers on how to interpret their dreams by using traditional Native American techniques such as meditation.

Beryl Beare, *Dreams and Destinies.* North Dighton, MA: JG Press, 1995. A book that claims to teach readers how to use their dreams to enhance their creativity and increase their ability to solve problems.

Kelly Bulkeley, ed., *Dreams.* New York: Pulgrave, 2001. A collection of essays concerning the religious, cultural, and psychological dimensions of dreams and dreaming.

Robert Crookall, *The Study and Practice of Astral Projection.* New Hyde Park, NY: University Books, 1966. A collection of experiences by those who claim to have had out-of-body experiences under a variety of circumstances, including during sleep and dreams.

Gayle Delaney, *All About Dreams.* San Francisco: HarperSanFrancisco, 1998. A study of dreams, what they are, what they mean, and how to utilize their power by the author of several books on dreams and the founder of the Association for the Study of Dreams.

William C. Dement, *The Promise of Sleep.* New York: Dell, 1999. A book about sleep, dreams, and the harmful effects experienced by people who do not get enough sleep. Written by the founder and director of the Stanford University Sleep Research Center.

Sigmund Freud, *The Interpretation of Dreams.* Trans. A.A. Brill. New York: Modern Library, 1994. A groundbreaking study of dreams and their meaning by the father of psychoanalysis.

David Gallup, *Aristotle on Sleep and Dreams.* Warminster, UK: Aris & Phillips, 1996. A translation and analysis of the three short books the classical Greek philosopher wrote about dreams in the fourth century B.C.

Patricia Garfield, *Creative Dreaming.* New York: Ballantine Books, 1974. A book that instructs people on methods for controlling, planning, and taking inspiration from their dreams.

————, *The Healing Power of Dreams.* New York: Fireside Book, 1991. A book that claims that dream power can keep people healthy and help heal sickness and disease.

J. Allan Hobson, *The Dreaming Brain.* New York: Basic Books, 1988. A scientific account of dreaming and dream theories by a professor of psychiatry at Harvard Medical School.

Stuart Holroyd, *Dream Worlds.* Garden City, NY: Doubleday, 1976. An examination of dreams from many viewpoints, from the scientific to the supernatural.

Joseph Katz, *Dreams Are Your Truest Friends.* New York: Simon & Schuster, 1975. A book that lists the many cultural influences dreams have had on society throughout the ages and explains how people can use their dreams to improve their lives.

Stephen LaBerge, *Lucid Dreaming.* New York: Ballantine Books, 1990. A study of lucid dreams by the pioneer in the field, with instructions for individuals who want to learn to consciously control their dreams.

James R. Lewis, *The Dream Encyclopedia.* Detroit: Visible Ink Press, 1995. A comprehensive study of all aspects of dreaming, including interpretation and religious and cultural references.

Naphtali Lewis, ed., *The Interpretation of Dreams and Portents.* Toronto: Hakkert, 1976. A collection of ancient dream interpretations and lore, from the Mesopotamians to the Greeks. Also includes predictions made by astrologers, fortune-tellers, and others.

John E. Mack, *Nightmares and Human Conflict.* Boston: Little, Brown, 1970. A psychological study that interprets dreams and nightmares.

Morris Edward Opler, *An Apache Life-Way.* New York: Cooper Square, 1965. First printed in 1941, this book has hundreds of quotes from elder Apache pertaining to ancient customs involving childhood, marriage, social relations, and spiritual beliefs.

Gyatrul Rinpoche, *Ancient Wisdom.* Ithaca, NY: Snow Lion Publications, 1993. A book that explains the history and techniques of meditation, dream yoga, and other Eastern religious practices.

D. Scott Rogo, *NAD: A Study of Some Unusual "Other-World" Experiences.* New Hyde Park, NY: University Books, 1970. Nad is Sanskrit for astral phenomena and well represents this collection of astral travel stories by a member of the American Society for Psychical Research.

Sandra Shulman, *Nightmares*. New York: Macmillan, 1979. An exploration into the world of scary dreams and how they have been used as artistic inspiration by painters, poets, and musicians.

Robert Van de Castle, *Our Dreaming Mind*. New York: Ballantine Books, 1994. An examination of the vital role dreams have played throughout history by the director of the Sleep and Dream Laboratory at the University of Virginia Medical School.

Fred Alan Wolf, *The Dreaming Universe*. New York: Simon & Schuster, 1994. A study of the psychological and scientific elements of dreaming.

Internet Sources

Ramesh Balsekar, "Importance of Dreams in the Mystical Process." www.plotinus. com. A site that explores the complex beliefs of Tibetan dream yoga.

BuddhaNet, "Life of Buddha: (Part One) Queen Maya's Dream," 2003. www. buddhanet.net. The story of the birth of Buddha as described on a website dedicated to Buddhist studies.

Robert Todd Carroll, "Lucid Dreaming," The Skeptic's Dictionary, 2002. www.skepdic.com. A web page from The Skeptic's Dictionary website that calls into doubt the dream state known as lucid dreaming.

———, "Psychoanalysis and Sigmund Freud," The Skeptic's Dictionary, 2002. www.skepdic.com. Another web page from The Skeptic's Dictionary website that questions the scientific validity of psychoanalysis and Freud's interpretation of dreams.

Central Premonitions Registry, 1995. http://mainportals.com. A website where people can record what they feel are predictive dreams, and where the dreams can be accessed in case they come true.

"Course in Lucid Dreaming/Astral Travelling," October 11, 1999. The Cosmic Connection. http://homepage. powerup.com.au. An Australian site that offers dream workshops in various paranormal fields.

Preston E. Dennett, "Premonitions of Disaster," *Atlantis Rising Magazine*. www.atlantisrising.com. An investigation into the validity of premonitions of famous disasters throughout the twentieth century.

Discoveryhealth.com, "Sleep and Dreams," January 10, 2003. http://health.discovery. com. A site about the importance of dreams to the ancient Egyptians.

"Dream Therapy," NursingPower.net. www.reikinurse.com. A site that recommends methods for dream incubation, with references to books on the topic.

Martin Ebon, "Mark Twain's 'Mental Telegraphy,'" New Paradigm Books, 2001. www.newpara.com. A website detailing Mark Twain's well-known interest in psychic phenomenon.

Craig Hamilton-Parker, "Titanic Coincidences," www.spiritualists.org. A website that compares the *Titanic* shipwreck to unfortunate problems encountered by film crews and actors while making the blockbuster movie of the same name.

Lynne Levitan and Stephen LaBerge, "Out-of-Body Experiences and Lucid Dreams," Lucidity Institute, March 1991. www.lucidity.com. A site explaining astral travel by renowned researchers in the field of lucid dreaming.

Lucidity Insitute, "Lucid Dreaming FAQ," January 16, 2003. www.lucidity.com. A site that explains lucid dreaming and the positive effects of utilizing lucid dreaming techniques.

"Native American Dream Catchers," Native American Dreams, 2003. http://groups.msn.com. A site dedicated to Native American culture, society, and spirituality.

Joe Nickell, "Paranormal Lincoln," Lincoln and the Paranormal: Investigative Files, May/June 1999. www.csicop.org. An article that attempts to disprove belief in Abraham Lincoln's prophetic dreams, his alleged ghost stalking the White House, and other paranormal phenomena associated with the sixteenth president.

Alice Ouzounian, "Tibetan Dream Yoga," December 30, 2002. www.plotinus.com. A site with information about the ancient Tibetan practice of dream yoga, along with general information about dreams and dreaming.

Henry Reed, "Incubating Dreams Solves Problems," Intuitive-Connections Network, February 17, 2003. www.intuitive-connections.net. A site about problem solving during dreams based on scientific research conducted on dream incubation.

Jacob Schwartz, "Can Dreams Preview the Future," The New Age Directory. www.newage-directory.com. A site with various types of premonitory dreams and the kinds of situations where they occur.

Anita Stratos, "Perchance to Dream," Tour Egypt. www.touregypt.net. A site that explores the importance of dream interpretation to the ancient Egyptians.

Craig Webb, "Harvesting Dreamland," The Dream Foundation. www.dreams.ca. A site that features information about recalling and incubating dreams in order to improve one's life.

Index

Picture Credits

About the Author

Stuart A. Kallen is the author of more than 150 nonfiction books for children and young adults. He has written on topics ranging from the theory of relativity to the history of rock and roll. In addition, Mr. Kallen has written award-winning children's videos and television scripts. In his spare time, Mr. Kallen is a singer/song-writer/guitarist in San Diego, California.